"Cyndi Parker puts Jesus in his place and tir the story of Jesus to life by revealing when whom he lived."

—John A. Beck, Making Bible Geography Meaningful

"Cyndi Parker has produced a reliable, accessible, and interesting introduction to Jesus within his canonical, historical, geographical, political, and cultural context. Readers will become aware of how their own cultural assumptions drive so much of their biblical interpretation, and they will gain a deeper and more accurate understanding of Jesus and his world. She has packed a lot into this relatively concise book, for which readers will be extremely grateful!"

—Roy E. Ciampa, Armstrong Chair of Religion, Samford University

"This book by Cyndi Parker is a concise but accurate read of the history, geography, and theology of the Bible. Professor Parker has taken large sections of biblical text and molded them into a cohesive narrative. As a Pro-Torah Messianic, I was glad to see Ms. Parker's book take seriously the Hebrew Scriptures and their contribution to the New Testament. I am enthusiastic about the appeal of this book across many theological boundaries. This book is loaded with attention to the importance of biblical geography and Ms. Parker is on the cutting edge of that frontier. I plan on using this book for small-group meetings and encourage others to do the same. Thanks to Cyndi Parker for writing this book. I plan on recommending this book to everyone."

—Brent Emery, Teaching Rabbi of Beit Tefillah

"Most people are malnourished in their understanding of how the geography, history, and cultural context of the biblical world impact their reading of the Scriptures—especially the Gospels. Subsequently, they don't realize how much they're missing. This is why Cyndi's book is such a remarkable resource. Brilliantly researched and accessibly written, this book will dramatically enhance your understanding of Jesus' life and ministry. Never again will you read the Gospels the same."

—Brad Gray, founder, Walking the Text

"This book entices the reader into the whole story of Scripture through the land and key figures that are found within. Written in engaging style and full of insight and depth, this book allows both student and layperson to walk into the story of Scripture with ease."

—Sarah Harris, New Testament Lecturer, Carey Baptist College

"Cyndi Parker offers us a refreshing view of Jesus—one that embraces him as a rabbi, coworker, and friend immersed in the multifaceted world of first-century Judaism. Written in a sweeping, conversational style, this book guides us through the interplay of history, geography, religion, and worldview that shaped the hopes, aspirations, and real-world nitty-gritty of Jews in the time of the Gospels. Parker brings the acumen of a scholar, the sensitivity of a teacher, and the heart of a believer—all honed by years of engaging the reality of the Gospels in Jerusalem, Judea, Samaria, and Galilee. Read this book. It will help you know Jesus better."

—Paul H. Wright, President, Jerusalem University College

"Parker reminds us that the Bible is not just a text to read, it is a whole world to explore. For many years, she has led classes and tours through the physical sites of biblical history. Now she lends her expertise to help readers encounter Jesus in a fresh way through better understanding the history, culture, and geography of Jesus' life and ministry. This is a great way to enhance your understanding of the story of Jesus in the Gospels."

—Nijay K. Gupta, Professor of New Testament, Northern Seminary

"If we would understand Jesus, we have to understand his world. That is the premise of this vividly illuminating book by a gifted scholar and teacher and expert on the land and literature of ancient Israel. Cyndi Parker brings to life treasures from the lived experience of people in the time of Jesus, factors of history, geography, tradition, and custom that provided their mental furniture and the shape of their hopes and fears. She then shows by skilled interpretation how an appreciation of these things can be transformative for our reading of the Gospels."

—Gordon McConville, Professor Emeritus of Old Testament Theology
University of Gloucestershire

"In this first-rate work, Cyndi Parker expertly draws together the fruit of her years of vibrant instruction in the Land of Israel with her wide-ranging knowledge of biblical and extrabiblical texts. It's all about identity, place, and connections—the first-century Jews of Jesus' day were firmly connected with their past. The Torah revealed at Sinai was to shape their communal life in the land; in turn, the land shaped them and their stories. The network of connections is rich: definitive events in Israel's history embodied in the life of Jesus; agriculturally based festivals enriched by the words of Jesus; familiar names, such as Capernaum and Tiberias, lodged in the significant geopolitical contexts in which Jesus taught—and that is just a taste of the sumptuous fare in this book."

—Elaine Phillips
Distinguished Professor Emeritus of Biblical Studies, Gordon College

"For anyone looking for a new take on familiar Scriptures, Cyndi Parker offers a refreshing approach for better understanding the biblical narrative in its original context. To the beautiful picture of how God has worked in this world, this book offers a lovely framework that brings all of the varying elements of that picture into better focus. Students of biblical history, pastors searching for a winsome way to interpret the life and words of Jesus to their listeners, and any who simply wish to become better Bible readers will benefit from the careful work Cyndi Parker has done here in uncovering the multiple layers that encompass the timeless witness of God's word."

—C. Chappell Temple, Lead Pastor, Christ Church (UMC) Sugar Land, Texas

"If you don't want to have your Western colloquial caricatures of Jesus dismantled, don't read this book! On the other hand, if you're itching to look at Jesus through the lens of the world in which he really lived, you'll love this book. Dr. Parker roots her study of Jesus in the deep soil of the Hebrew scriptures. From there, she puts our sandals directly on the soil where we experience the geographical, agricultural, and sociopolitical distinctives of the land where Jesus lived. A must-read for Bible students, teachers, and pastors who know that context matters."

—Brian Buhler, spiritual director, homiletical coach
The Christian and Missionary Alliance, Canada

Encountering *Jesus* in the
Real World *of the* Gospels

— CYNDI PARKER —

HENDRICKSON
PUBLISHERS

an imprint of Hendrickson Publishing Group

Encountering Jesus in the Real World of the Gospels

© 2021 Cyndi Parker

Published by Hendrickson Publishers
an imprint of Hendrickson Publishing Group
Hendrickson Publishers, LLC
P. O. Box 3473
Peabody, Massachusetts 01961-3473
www.hendricksonpublishinggroup.com

ISBN 978-1-68307-310-9

Printed in the United States of America

First Printing — February 2021

Library of Congress Control Number: 2020949886

Maps by Cristalle Kishi; base maps by Michael Schmeling, www.aridocean.com.

In loving memory of Vernon Alexander (1975–2020), who loved the physical context of Jesus almost as much as the character of Jesus. I miss you, my dear friend.

Contents

ILLUSTRATIONS

FIGURES

Acknowledgments

Traveling in the physical land where so many biblical events took place changed my understanding of Scripture. I owe a debt of gratitude to the land that holds so many memories and challenges me to identify and reconsider some of my assumptions about history. Thank you, Dr. Paul Wright, for helping me learn to see the land as a significant character in the biblical narratives, and thank you to all the students and participants in my educational groups who asked questions, challenged ideas, and sharpened my communication skills.

This book began as a conversation with Danielle Parish. The two of us share a love for teaching about Jesus in the land where he grew up. Although we both observe expressions of surprise on people's faces as they experience places like Galilee and Jerusalem, Danielle is the one who understood the need for a book like this one. I am grateful for her vision, and I hope that she will be proud of this finished manuscript.

Whenever I wrestled with wrapping words around complex ideas, Mindelynn Young, Lisa Nickel, and Kendra Denlinger patiently read versions of each chapter and made helpful comments on how I could express concepts more clearly. I love their curious minds and am glad to have such brilliant women in my corner.

My deepest expressions of gratitude, however, go to Kathy and Scott Parker who are known to me as Mom and Dad. They read every version of all my writings and then drew me into conversations that pushed beyond my writings to explore ideas more fully. My parents are bright lights of encouragement when frustrations dimmed my way.

INTRODUCTION

I did not grow up with a burning desire to visit the land of the Bible. I did not think it mattered. Then toward the end of my seminary studies, I began to feel restless. In my classes, I wrestled with theological issues, which were interesting, but I had a sense there was something else important that I was missing.

Based on a professor's suggestion, I decided to spend my last year of seminary in Israel. That was when I realized that what I was missing was experiencing the *locatedness* of the biblical stories. I discovered that I loved standing on the ruins of ancient cities and imagining the experienced reality of the people who lived there long ago, and I began to recognize the humanity of the people in the Bible instead of thinking of them as only carriers of a theological lesson. Being in the land gave me a new lens through which to study God's revolutionary story to engage humanity and to mend the broken relationship between the divine, humans, and the created world. Learning and experiencing the context of the biblical world was fascinating enough to convince me to remain in Israel for several years, teaching other people to engage the geography, history, and cultural context of the Bible.

During one of those classes, I took a group to Bethlehem to explore the rich historical and geographical context of both King David and Jesus. In the final hours of the day, I sat on a carved, wooden pew in a beautiful Catholic church. A sweet student turned to me and whispered, "Is this the church Jesus came to as a child?" I paused for a moment as thoughts passed rapid-fire through my head. Should I explain that neither the church nor Christianity existed at the time of Jesus? Do I remind the student that Jesus was Jewish and therefore went to synagogues, because churches didn't yet exist? Do I point out that Jesus grew up in Nazareth, and we were definitely not in Nazareth? If I remember correctly, I took the easy way out and simply leaned over and answered, "No."

The student's question revealed her limited understanding of the historic reality of Jesus. The Jesus she knew emerged from her own context and belonged in the large, beautiful, Christian churches of the Western world. But she is not alone in her assumptions about Jesus. In Israel, I teach students of all ages and with all levels of biblical knowledge. In the beginning of every course, students are struck by how different the real contexts of the Gospel stories are from how they imagined them. They then become enthralled with the process of discovering an accurate picture of Jesus contextualized in his historical landscape.

Jesus' ministry was exciting because he was the continuation, the climax even, of God's long history of interacting with and revealing himself to humanity. The Western church sometimes considers the Old Testament and the New Testament as separate and independent entities. However, without understanding the whole story of God and how Jesus fits into it, we are not engaging the full depth and richness of the Gospels. If we are to understand the historical Jesus, then we need to start at the beginning and recognize that Jesus had a mission connected to the Old Testament narratives, which in turn occurred on the stage of a very specific landscape that played a great role in the narratives and the way in which they were recorded.

Modern readers who think of the Gospels as self-contained histories of Jesus do not ask the significant contextual questions that have massive implications for interpreting the Gospels. For instance, the writings of the Old Testament are written in Hebrew (with some Aramaic) but the Gospels are written in Greek. Why is that? God's people in the Old Testament are called Israelites, but in the Gospels, they are called Jews. Is that change significant? In the Old Testament, the Israelites have a kingdom with political borders. In the Gospels, the Jews live scattered throughout the Roman Empire. So, what did concepts of the kingdom of God mean for the Jewish people who did not have a kingdom? The Old Testament focuses on the temple in Jerusalem, but the Gospels mention synagogues. Where did synagogues come from, and what is their relationship with the temple? The Judaism represented in the New Testament is not the same as the Israelite religion in the Old Testament. But how is it different, and why did it evolve? The Gospels also mention people such as the Herodians, Pharisees, and Sadducees. Who are these people, and how are they different from the crowds of people who followed Jesus? These are all important contextual questions to ask before diving into the life and teachings of Jesus.

Misunderstanding Context: Eastern versus Western Mind-Set

One challenge for Western Christians when reading the Gospels is coming to the realization that the way we perceive the world is quite different from how first-century Jews saw it.[1] To specifically engage this issue, I like to take students into a shop in the Old City of Jerusalem to talk with Dove and Moshe Kempinski. They are Orthodox Jewish brothers who offer a hospitable place in which to engage Christian-Jewish dialogue. When explaining the difference of perspective between the Western visitors in their shop and the Eastern worldview of the locals, Moshe tells groups that there are no thirty-year-old Jews nor are there thirty-year-old Palestinians. And then he pauses. Inevitably, a look of confusion washes over everyone's face as they think through their day and all the people they saw. Of course, there are thirty-year-olds in the city! Moshe then continues, "They are all three thousand years old." In a simple sentence, Moshe captures a significant difference between Western and Eastern mind-sets.

The Western mind-set evolved from Greco-Roman abstract concepts of philosophy and data in which emotions are separated from the individual.[2] Children are taught to be independent thinkers and true to themselves without being influenced by a group. An individual is told they can make anything of themselves, regardless of their context or background. People with a Western mind-set face the future as the great unknown into which they are eager to run. They do not want to be hindered or held back by the past. A Western mind-set states that the belief of what is right and wrong is internally cultivated. Choices are for the individual alone to make. Therefore, people with a Western mind-set analyze Jesus' teachings for a linear set of logical data points. Jesus died and rose again *for the individual*, and the individual's belief in Jesus is a *private* decision.

An Eastern mind-set is concerned with relationships, networks, and narratives. For them, true theology is embodied in *actions* and not in abstract ideas.[3] Collectivism is prioritized, which means value is placed on family and community over the individual. People with an Eastern mind-set will face the past, which is known, and walk backward into the future, which is unknown. They understand that their history and family connections got them to where they are in the present, and they bring their whole past into conversations about the present. Children are taught to avoid shame and maintain honor for the sake of the whole family, whose reputation is more important than the individual's. For those with an Eastern mind-set, there are no such things as the Western concepts of "rugged individualism" or "private Christianity."[4]

This is why many of Jesus' actions and words stirred up a significant response from Jewish leaders in the community. The Jewish identity was strongly anchored to the collective participation in festivals, circumcision, food, and the single temple in Jerusalem. When Jesus healed people on the Sabbath or said the temple would be destroyed, people heard his words as potentially shaking the very identity of the community. Jewish leaders were concerned for the fabric of society, not necessarily the individual's choice to follow Jesus.

I point out the difference between the Eastern and Western mind-sets not to make a statement about which is better or worse but to highlight the fact that there are differing ways of organizing priorities and making sense of the world. We create blinders that limit our understanding of Scripture when we are not aware of how we culturally and intuitively see the world and how it is different from the context within which the Gospels were written.

Jesus, his disciples, and normal first-century Jews understood their world through narrative and symbols. The sacred scrolls that the Jews valued and in which they found hope were a literary tapestry that included threads of historical persons, prophetic images, and historical precedent that provided recognizable patterns. Remember from the story above how Moshe said modern Jews were all three thousand years old? The same concept applies to first-century Jews. They used the patterns of Scripture to understand their current events. The Gospel writers subtly point to many of these replicated patterns to explain why Jesus made sense as the Jewish Messiah.

Theological and Cultural Divide

You may wonder why imagining Jesus in his historical context is not as intuitive for us as we think it should be. How did the modern church lose the connection between Jesus and his Jewish context when all of the first Christians were Jews? There are several contributing factors, but I will briefly discuss just the political and cultural reasons here.[5]

The church was birthed as a Jewish movement with Jerusalem as the primary seat of leadership.[6] The first Christians attended synagogues and visited the temple in Jerusalem. Those who followed Jesus essentially became another branch of Judaism.[7] The first chapters of the book of Acts portray the growing rift between the Jews and the Jewish Christians (Acts 3:1–8:3). The Jewish Christians fled from Jerusalem under threat of persecution. In 66 CE, the Jews started a revolt that attempted to overthrow Roman rule, while the Jewish Christians did not participate. This amplified the animosity between them and the Jews who hoped for national independence.

The revolt led to the destruction of the temple, which in turn initiated a significant time of transformation for Jewish thought.[8] An intensive restructuring of Judaism was necessary after the rituals of the temple were no longer possible. An infamous meeting took place at Jamnia in which leading Jewish scholars gathered with the hope of preserving Jewish traditions, rituals, and identity. They recognized that their new context demanded an eradication of the existing pluralism within Judaism, otherwise Judaism would not survive. With hopes of solidifying the longevity of Jewish identity, the leaders wrote an official policy rejecting all "sectarians, detractors, and defectors"[9]—in other words, "those who severed all ties with their people."[10] The statement applied to many groups that were designated as heretical, and it is ambiguous to what extent the Jews at that time considered Christians to be in that category.

Although the rift between the Jewish Christians and the Jews had been growing for some time, the official divide happened during the second Jewish revolt against Rome (132–135 CE). A Jewish leader named Bar Kokhba was upheld as the Messiah. He successfully unified the Jewish people in the resistance movement, but the Jewish Christians simply could not support such messianic claims. They refused to fight with Bar Kokhba against the Romans. After the revolt, the ambiguous status of Christians among the Jewish community was gone. Christians were now considered heretics.

In the meantime, Paul set out on his missionary journeys throughout the Roman Empire. He taught Jewish people in synagogues, but he also engaged Gentiles in the public square. His journeys were successful, and more and more Gentiles joined the Christian movement. The influx of Gentiles prompted the earliest Jewish Christian leaders to decide if the Gentiles needed to become Jewish before being accepted into the church. Amid much debate, the leaders decided at the Jerusalem Council that conversion to Judaism was not necessary for Gentiles to turn to God (Acts 15:1–21).

The mission of Jesus, which was originally understood as a continuation of the original Israelite narratives, was translated into Greco-Roman philosophical, Western thought. This jump into a different worldview was extraordinary. Slowly, the Jewish Christians were outnumbered by the Gentile Christians, who had a different cultural background from the Jews. People in the Roman world did not understand Jewish history, nor were they concerned with preserving Jewish identity. Gentiles did not have the same sacred texts that created expectations about a messiah, and they did not identify with the practice of going to synagogue, celebrating Jewish festivals, or eating kosher food. The Gentiles who did not understand the rich background of Jesus, as it was rooted in the Hebrew Scriptures, disregarded that to which they did not culturally relate.

The church slowly severed the connection between Jesus and his Jewish world, and over time, Christianity became de-Judaized.[11] Christians defined themselves with non-Jewish terminology, using Greek terms and ultimately Greek philosophy to explain their beliefs. Christians spoke of themselves as the "new Israel." Christians deemphasized observance of the Sabbath and encouraged gatherings on Sunday (instead of Saturday) to remember Jesus' resurrection. Jews had an increasingly difficult time responding to a Christian message that required them to reject the Sabbath, which they viewed as a rejection of the Mosaic law. Ironically, as we saw, while the early days of the Christian movement necessitated a debate of whether Gentiles needed to become Jewish before following God, as the movement grew, the debate turned to if Jews needed to reject the Jewishness of their past to belong to the church.

This is only a general explanation of how the church lost its ability to understand Jesus in his historical context. But these theological and cultural divides cannot be underestimated. The modern Western church evolved out of the context of the Roman Empire. That context led to the historic church's assumption that the Israelite Torah (or the Pentateuch) was "a legalistic foil from which Jesus has delivered us."[12] That assumption lingers even to this day. The theological and cultural divide between Christianity and Judaism is centuries old, so we have quite a bit of work to do if we are going to override ingrained cultural assumptions to gain a richer understanding of Scripture and God's persistent love for humanity throughout history.

Recontextualizing Jesus

To understand why others perceived Jesus as both fascinating and problematic, we need to explore the people and places surrounding him. I want to stoke your curiosity about information that is sometimes assumed to be normal in the Gospels. Therefore, the first part of this book will cultivate an understanding of the historical events that took place *before* Jesus was born in Bethlehem. We want to build the stage, understand the unspoken social undercurrents, and become aware of who occupied positions of power. We will focus on literature, history, geography, and the evolution of cultural ideas. Since the Gospels do not explicitly lay these details out for us, we will use other sources to help us.[13] Each of these elements enhances the complexity and beauty that is present in the Gospels but often missed with a cursory reading.

With that foundation in place, the second half of the book will examine significant phases of Jesus' life. We want to encounter Jesus, the disciples, and the crowds as real people in a real place at a time vastly different from our own. After doing the initial work in the first part of this book, we can then approach the Gospels with new eyes and a renewed curiosity. Although we are retelling the narratives of Jesus' life, death, and resurrection, we are actually engaging the entire narrative of God's interaction with humanity throughout time.

Since the focus of this book is on the context of Jesus, technical issues of when, how, or by whom the Gospel narratives were written are beyond the scope of this particular project. Nor can we develop a complete theological portrait of each individual Gospel. There are many other books that can help you achieve those aims, and I will include them in a recommended reading list at the end of the book. My goal is to whet your appetite and create enough intrigue to motivate you to dig deeper into the Gospel stories.

In the following chapters, we will take the Gospel narratives and anchor them into that real time and place and then listen for the echoes from the Old Testament narratives. This will be the time to ask new questions about a story that might seem familiar to you and therefore challenge yourself to hear Jesus' message afresh. With this book, please allow me to invite you into a process that will allow you to expand what you know about Jesus!

Part One

CONTEXT MATTERS

1

EDEN TO EXILE

If I were to ask you where in the Bible the Gospel story begins, how would you answer? If you said it began in Matthew 1, you would not be alone; but I offer a counterargument. I am convinced that the Gospel story does not begin with the birth of Jesus but with the beginning of Genesis. The Gospel writers thought this as well. The Gospel of Matthew, for instance, makes initial claims about the significance of Jesus in the first chapter, using a genealogy that identifies the larger story to which Jesus belonged. Matthew sets the stage for the reader before explaining the magnificent events that took place in Jesus' life. God was faithful to his people in the past and continues to be faithful through Jesus. Remember, we are reading a document written from an Eastern worldview. This is not a story of one man but of a whole people group. Only because Jesus belonged to the Israelite story did his role as the Jewish Messiah make sense. Each of the Gospel writers claimed that Jesus' teachings and actions, along with his death and resurrection, were the continuation and climax of the ancient biblical story.[1] We should therefore follow the Gospel writers' lead and not approach these books as if they told a new narrative disconnected from the history that came before them.

Unfortunately, many Christian communities are unfamiliar with the particularities of the Old Testament. Granted, reading such an ancient text takes extra effort on the part of the reader. Modern readers have difficulty feeling connected to a foreign place or identifying with people who have unfamiliar social norms. Some readers simplify the task by choosing favorite figures for a character study. Others may look through the book of Proverbs for easily applied wisdom sayings. Without examining the larger narrative, untangling the ancient customs, or observing patterns that emerge in multiple books, Old Testament stories end up being like bubbles in our minds, floating in theological space independently of one another. Here is the David and Goliath story, and there is the story of Saul meeting the witch of Endor. Joshua fights a battle at Jericho, and Solomon is given wisdom. The bubbles do not relate to one another, nor are they anchored in the physical land. Therefore, the stories have significance only in themselves and not in what they contribute to the larger historical narrative. If we study the Old Testament this way, then it is equally easy to identify Jesus as another independent bubble—a story disconnected from all the others. This is not at all how the Gospels were designed to be read.

Christian communities teach that Jesus was fully human and fully divine, but if we are not careful, we are in danger of assuming that means he came as an infant with a fully formed understanding of his mission and purpose. Such a conclusion dismisses the human experience and wipes away the deep mystery of the incarnation. It is hard for us to imagine Jesus as an infant who nursed at Mary's breast and had to learn to speak. So how did Jesus gain insight into his life's mission? The Gospels suggest that it was a gradual process and that throughout his youth, he continued to grow in wisdom and in understanding (Luke 2:40, 52).

How did Jesus gain knowledge about God's goals and purposes for his people? The answers came from the Old Testament (or Hebrew Bible). As Jesus grew from infancy to young adulthood, like many Jewish children, he would have been immersed in Jewish texts.[2] By the time he entered his public ministry, the rich story of God's involvement in human affairs would have crystalized his own identity and mission.

For hundreds of years, the Jews studied, reflected on, and memorized the documents that told them about their history as God's people. The confidence of the Jewish community for their hope for the future stemmed from knowing what God did for them in the past.

> Jesus and his first followers were Jews whose symbolic world was shaped by Israel's Scripture: their ways of interpreting the world and their hopes for God's saving action were fundamentally conditioned by the biblical stories of God's dealings with the people Israel.[3]

So, when Jesus began his public ministry, the Jewish leaders and the crowds of people evaluated Jesus' actions and teachings through the rich lens of the

Hebrew narrative. People identified Jesus as authoritative, or as problematic, based on how he affirmed or challenged the text.

The Gospel writers did something similar. These writers documented the events of Jesus' life from the perspective *after* Jesus' ministry, death, and resurrection. In other words, they had the luxury of distance to look again at Scripture and to recognize how Jesus' life shed additional light on earlier events. In looking backward, the Gospel writers identified patterns that connected historical writings and events with Jesus' life. Events or prophecies from the past may not have been noticed as significant in the moment, but the Gospel writers saw them glimmer in new ways in light of Jesus. Such is the value of hindsight and of the Holy Spirit making all this clear to them. But the realization of the brilliance in Scripture goes both ways. The events of Jesus' life became more dynamic when viewed in light of the past.[4] The Gospel writers therefore invite the reader to understand Jesus and to conclude that he truly was the Messiah *through the lens of the Hebrew narrative.*

If the Gospel writers, after knowing Jesus and ascertaining the importance of his life, thought that the good news of the gospel could stand on its own without the Old Testament, then they would have left it out. But all of them interpret Jesus as belonging to the long historical narrative of the Israelites. They understood that the patterns in the narratives revealed the character of God throughout Israel's history, and they specifically drew attention to these patterns as proof of who Jesus was. Since the Gospel writers assumed their readers knew the Israelite texts, we will be better served in our study of the Gospels to remind ourselves of Israel's history. If we approach the Gospels with amnesia about the Israelite story, then we will not recognize the details these writers use to craft their narratives about Jesus' significance.

Therefore, before we dive into a study on who Jesus was in his physical and cultural context, let us review the content of the writings that he and his community considered sacred. Our goal is to understand the narrative continuity between Jesus and Israel's Scriptures. Please keep in mind that for practical purposes, this is only an overview, so I run the risk of oversimplifying an intricate collection of texts. I feel immense pressure here as an Old Testament scholar! Although there is so much more I want to tell you, my purpose here will focus on highlighting some of the people, images, and patterns from the sacred text that Jesus held so dearly.

In the Beginning

In the beginning of God's act of creation, the Spirit of God fluttered over the watery void of chaos and divided it to bring order, design, and beauty. God looked at his artwork and called it good. God then created humans and invited them to participate in his ordered world by guarding and protecting this beauty.

The creation stories in Genesis 1 and 2 are poetic, beautiful, and breathtaking in the scope and the implications of what it means for beauty to beget beauty, for all humans to be made in God's image, and for the relationship God desired to have with his creation. God dwelt with humans, and those humans lived in harmony with one another other and with the garden-land around them.

When Adam and Eve questioned God's instructions (Gen. 2:17–18) and made their own decisions about what was good (Gen. 3:6), they shattered the beauty of the created order. The consequence of their actions resulted in expulsion from the place where they had experienced an intimate relationship with God, a harmonious relationship with one another, and abundant sustenance from the land. Even though the disruption was the humans' fault, God promised to be actively involved in fixing the problem and restoring all of the relationships (God–people–creation) in a healthy manner.

The first three chapters of Genesis give the reader a picture of God's vision for taking disordered chaos and creating extraordinary beauty. These chapters explain the ideal connection between God, humanity, and the natural world. This ideal then becomes a significant theme throughout the rest of Scripture. Sure, the human choice to question God resulted in brokenness, but the brokenness is not the beginning of the narrative. The narrative begins with God's goodness, his desire for order, the recognition that places matter and that God desires human participation in beauty. The first chapters of Genesis also communicate the death-like consequence of being expelled from the relationships and place in which humans were designed to be.

The Israelite origin story is designed to engage the age-old, existential human questions: Where did we come from? Why are we here? What are we doing? Why are things wrong in the world? How do I relate to the divine? Genesis answers with a *narrative*, and that narrative is about a singular God creating beauty and then creating humanity from within that beauty.

God gave responsibility to humans to work and protect what he made; he designed them to be in fellowship with him. The narratives explain why things in the world seem broken, but they also provide hope that the one who created perfectly in the beginning is also the one who can take what was broken and restore that beauty.

Noah's epic flood story is, in a sense, another origin story. When Genesis 1 and Genesis 6–9 are read together, similarities emerge. The waters that God parted in Genesis 1 crashed in on each other in Genesis 7. In Genesis 8, God caused a wind to blow and the waters parted. Dry land appeared, and Noah's descendants were given another chance at dwelling in a place of beauty where right-relatedness between God, humans, and nature was a reality. In the first eleven chapters of Genesis, patterns emerge around images of parted waters, exposed ground, and a new place where God and humans can dwell in harmony.

Although God promised not to flood the earth again, what confidence did Noah's descendants have that he would remain true to his word? To answer the question, we need to know that within the ancient Near Eastern cultural context, family, relationships, and symbols were of utmost importance. Individuals (or possibly clans or nations) who did not share the same bloodline used covenants to enter into an agreement. Those covenants required each entity to treat the other entity like family. In effect, covenants were a common ancient Near Eastern way to create kinship lines where none previously existed. For example, a *parity* covenant was made between parties of similar authoritative status (thus creating "siblings" of each other), and a *suzerain-vassal* covenant was made between parties of unequal power (thus creating a parent-child relationship). So why did Noah and his family have confidence in God's promise? Because God did a remarkable thing: he created a covenant with them; God made Noah's family his kin.

A Chosen Family

In the ancient Near East, three essential aspects of life determined people's worldview: the gods they served, the family they were a part of, and the land to which they belonged. Those three elements formed the lens through which people understood authority, structured society, and established family identity. Keep this in mind as we move into Genesis 12.

Starting in Genesis 12:1, we see that God's plan to fix what was broken in the created order would come to pass through one family. God said to Abram, "Go forth from your country, and from your relatives and from your father's house to the land which I will show you."[5] Did you catch all that Abram would have to leave without receiving answers about the future? Country, extended family, and father's house. Think of how remarkable it would be for the original audience to hear this request from God. The instructions would seem almost absurd to the ancient audience. Abram's extended family network and the cherished family knowledge of their land shaped his identity. And yet, God asked him to leave behind all this to create a new reality.

Abram obeyed God, and in return, God changed Abram's name to Abraham and promised him a new land as an inheritance and a family with more descendants than the stars in the sky. In answer to Abraham's inevitable question about what guarantee he had that God's promise was trustworthy, God created a covenant with him. The narrative in Genesis 15 is almost as astounding as the instructions in Genesis 12. As soon as the reader hears God's command to bring animals and cut them in half (Gen. 15:9–10), the ancient audience would have recognized the action right away as the beginning of the covenant ceremony. In the ancient Near East, however, the weaker party normally walked between the bloody carcasses, inevitably kicking blood onto the hem of their garment. They would swear an oath that if they broke the covenant, then they would become like the animal carcasses. But in Genesis 15, Abraham does not pass through the carcasses; God does. God took full responsibility for the covenantal promises.

As we see in Genesis, God continued to work through Abraham's family, and within three generations (Isaac, Jacob, and Jacob's twelve sons), they multiplied exponentially. Then during Jacob's lifetime, a famine drove Abraham's descendants south to find sustenance in the fertile valleys of Egypt, where they continued to increase. But when their population growth became a threat to their host nation, the Egyptians enslaved the Israelites.

A Chosen Nation

After years of Egyptian oppression, God listened to the Israelite cries for help and raised up Moses to rescue the people. The various plagues represent the power of God going up against the power of Pharaoh. God won, and the Israelite people fled Pharaoh's oppressive rule. However, a body of water (the "Sea of Reeds" in the Hebrew) blocked their escape. With water on one side and Pharaoh's army approaching from behind, the Israelites were in an impossible situation. In the face of imminent danger, God provided a wind that parted the waters. Dry land appeared, and the people passed into safety. To the reader looking for patterns in the Hebrew narratives, the splitting of water to reveal dry ground that allowed the people to pass into a new beginning sounds like the creation and flood narratives, right? Keep your eyes open for more stories that fit this pattern.

The harsh environment of the wilderness was a challenging context for the Israelites, and yet the wilderness was where growth and restoration began. Those who fled Egypt as oppressed slaves had few resources, and yet they lacked nothing. God provided food, water, and navigation through the dry terrain. As they moved toward the land promised, Abraham's descendants were no longer under Egypt's oppression.

A new problem arose, however. How would a former group of slaves unite to form a nation? And how would those newly freed people find confidence that God would continue to provide for them? I venture that you already guessed that God made a covenant with them. Similar to the covenants with Noah's family and with Abraham's family, God initiated a new covenant with the Israelite people. When they set up camp at the base of Mount Sinai, Moses climbed to the top of the mountain and received the covenant. He took it to the people for them to agree on. That covenant formalized a personal relationship between God and his people. In contrast to the covenant made with Noah's family or with the patriarchs, this covenant was made between God and a *nation*. The Israelites were now a part of God's family and explicitly called the *son of God* (Exod. 4:22; Deut. 1:31).

God told the Israelites that he would dwell among them. Since the people lived in tents, so would God "live" in a tent. I love this next part in Exodus: God chose *artists* to be filled with wisdom and to create his abode (Exod. 31:3–4). The Creator God of Genesis continued to be a patron of the arts! The tabernacle was constructed in a highly symbolic way that represented both God's cohabitation with the people and also the sacred holiness of his residence. The tabernacle had a tripartite structure that included an open-air courtyard, the enclosed Holy Place, and the Holy of

Holies inside of the Holy Place. From the larger outer courtyard (framed with simple, common textiles) to the smallest room of the Holy of Holies (encased in costly materials and angelic designs), each space in the tabernacle was highly symbolic. While all of the Israelites were allowed to enter the outer courtyard, only the priests entered the Holy Place, and only one priest a year was allowed to enter the Holy of Holies where God's Spirit resided. The successively smaller spaces became more sacred as symbolized by the reduced size, quality of textiles, and restricted access.

Interestingly, when readers compare the tabernacle design with the description of Eden in Genesis 2, several parallels emerge.[6] Genesis 2 also reflects a tripartite design with the garden inside Eden and surrounded by ordinary space. The garden in Eden was like the Holy of Holies where God and humanity were together. The tasks given to the humans "to work" and "to keep" (or protect) the garden were the same tasks given to the priests in the tabernacle (Gen. 2:15; Num. 3:7–10). When the humans were exiled from the garden to the east, the tabernacle was always to face east to welcome those entering God's presence. It became a partial realization of the ideal beauty and right-relatedness of relationships lost in Eden. As the people of God journeyed to the place God promised to give to them, they had the presence of God in their midst.

An important and often overlooked aspect of the Israelite narrative so far is that God rescued the Israelites *before* they receive the law. God heard their cries, remembered his promise to Abraham, and brought the Israelites into freedom. The people did not do anything to earn God's deliverance; God freely gave it (Exod. 34:6–7a; Deut. 9:4). Therefore, when the law code was given to Israel through Moses, it was not to be the method through which the Israelites earned salvation. God had already saved them. The law code was designed to help the Israelites know how to respond properly to God. Even in the early interactions with God's people, we can see the similarity to what Paul says in Ephesians, "For it is by grace you have been saved through faith—and this not from yourselves, it is the gift of God" (Eph. 2:8). Likewise, Pinchas Lapide, a Jewish scholar, states,

> The rabbinate has never considered the Torah as a way of salvation to God. . . . [We Jews] regard salvation as God's exclusive prerogative, so we Jews are the advocates of "pure grace."[7]

God's election of Abraham and continued faithfulness to his descendants reflects God's gracious character and mercy.

The book of Deuteronomy was written as a set of final sermons that Moses gave to the Israelites before they entered into the land of their inheritance. Throughout the book, there is a common plea to the people to *remember*. Remember the character of their God. Remember who they are as his people. Interestingly, the people were not told to remember the laws! They were to rely on the memory of God acting first—out of love and faithfulness to the covenant promises he made—and that memory was the motivation to imitate his character and thus live out God's instructions.

At the core of the law are statements such as, "Hear, O Israel! The Lord our God, the Lord is one! Love the Lord your God with all your heart and with all your soul and with all your strength" (Deut. 6:4–5). This simple statement, also known as the *Shema,* functioned as the core affirmation of the Israelite faith. The statement is also the right response to the question, "If you could boil down the law to one sentence, what would it be?" (cf. Deut. 10:12–13). The answer? Love God with everything you have!

Before going further, I need to explain the Israelite law code a little more. Since God saved the Israelites before giving them the law, what role did the law serve in the Israelite community? Sometimes people disregard the Israelite law as a long series of oppressive commands that are impossible to fulfill. I hear students tell me how fortunate Christians are that Jesus came to replace the law with grace. Comments like that portray the speaker's opinion that the Israelite laws were an imposing and impossible set of rules. However, the Israelite Torah was less about restrictive laws and more about God's *teachings* about how to live fulfilled human lives in a God-honoring society. The Torah was "the revelation or teaching of the living God, who gave guidance and instruction for the benefit of his people."[8] God provided a set of guidelines to help the Israelites construct their observations, thoughts, and interactions with the world in such a way that they would reflect God's character to the nations of the world. The priority throughout the law is always on loving God and being like him over performing obligatory tasks, as is evident within the law code itself.

The Israelites, who were rescued from the "iron-smelting furnace" of oppression (Deut. 4:20), were about to enter the land of their inheritance. But how should they act within this place, especially when the only example of social structure they experienced was the bondage of slavery? The book of Deuteronomy casts a vision for the potential of what was possible: God's people living in a God-given place with God in their midst. For that vision to become a reality, however, the Israelites needed to follow God's teachings to create a God-honoring society. They needed to work toward harmonious relationships with one another and take care of the land that would support them and their descendants after them. The result would have an impact on the surrounding nations who would recognize the Israelites' wisdom and understanding—a people with God in their midst (Deut. 4:6–7). The vision that Deuteronomy paints is slightly reminiscent of Eden and just as beautiful.

The conclusion of Deuteronomy, though, offers a strict word of caution. The law represented wisdom, and breaking this law meant destroying the healthy relationships for which humans were created. The natural consequences of not following God's instructions would be separation from God, from one another, and from the land of their inheritance. And if you are developing eyes for a pattern here, you may notice that the consequences for breaking the covenant with God are the same as the consequences from Genesis 3, when the humans suffered the death-like effects of the broken relationships between people, land, and God.

After a forty-year delay in the wilderness, the Israelites finally stood on the edge of their land of inheritance. From the eastern side of the Jordan River, the people gazed at the land God had promised to give to Abraham's descendants. But to step foot in the land, they needed to pass through the waters. God caused the Jordan River to stop, dry ground appeared, and the people passed into a new land (Josh. 3:9–17). Oh wait. Did you catch that? Parting waters and dry ground. Does that remind you of anything? A pattern is definitely emerging!

The ecologically diverse land that Israel occupied becomes another character in the biblical narrative, albeit somewhat invisible to the modern reader who is not familiar with it. The contours of the land determined where the roads were built, how much rain was received, and what produce was grown. The land dictated the building materials used for homes and determined which communities had access to trade networks. The geography facilitated or complicated communication between neighbors and foreigners. Specific qualities of the land provided visual examples for complex theological ideas. Every narrative in the Bible was placed somewhere, and the land held the memory of those narratives. Readers of the Bible who are unfamiliar with the land tend to ignore this incredibly valuable character in the text. This is why we will explore the significance of the land in greater detail in the next chapter.

A Chosen King

The longer the Israelites resided in the land, the more complex their society became and the less viable it was for them to function as a loose coalition of tribes. Conflicts with surrounding people—such as the Edomites, Philistines, and Moabites—became more frequent. Turning away from the God who had always watched over them, the Israelites instead desired a human king to unify them, fight their battles, and lead them into a more prosperous era (1 Sam. 8:7–9, 19–20).

Saul was the first king of this Israelite coalition of tribes. He was "as handsome a young man as could be found anywhere in Israel, and he was a head taller than anyone else" (1 Sam. 9:2). Saul had the culturally acceptable look of an ideal leader and seemed to be a perfect candidate for king. Saul entered his position with gusto, but the historical narratives in 1 Samuel show the character flaws that threatened to crumble Saul's career. His faulty leadership, lack of courage, increased fear of losing the throne, and diminished obedience to God's instructions foretell the ultimate demise of his reign.

In contrast to Saul, David did not have the outer markings of the Israelites' idea of a successful king, being the youngest brother of a small family living in the village of Bethlehem. When the prophet Samuel went to Jesse's house to anoint the next king, Jesse assembled all of his sons except David. He was left out in the field! Even after Samuel anointed David, the young king-in-waiting shepherded the family's sheep while his older brothers fought in Saul's army. Strangely, David was anointed while Saul was still king and had to wait more than a decade until the time was right to assume the throne. But during that time, David proved himself to be a warrior and a leader. The narratives in 1 Samuel place Saul and David side by side, so that the contrast between them becomes apparent to the reader. Saul may have looked the part of king, but God saw that David had the true heart of a king (1 Sam. 16:7).

After Saul's death, David ruled over the southern tribes from Hebron. After eight years of negotiations, all of the tribes finally accepted him as king and David moved his capital city to Jerusalem.[9] Around this time, Israelite society was evolving from a tribal society to one with a centralized government. Under David's leadership, the kingdom expanded and experienced prosperity. By no means was David a perfect king, but he remained open to rebukes from the prophets. Despite his very human faults, David is remembered in Israelite literature as the ideal king who exemplified the heart of a God-appointed king.

David fought with surrounding nations and expanded Israelite boundaries. When he moved the tabernacle to the city of Jerusalem, he united the political role of the city with the spiritual role of tabernacle. When David finally enjoyed "rest from all of his enemies around him" (2 Sam. 7:1), he proposed to God that he would build a permanent house for him. "See now," David said, "Here I am, living in a house of cedar, while the ark of God remains in a tent" (2 Sam. 7:2). God's response to David addressed what may have been at the heart of David's initiative: the longevity of his reign.

> "Now I will make your name great. . . . And I will provide a place for my people Israel and will plant them so that they can have a home of their own and no longer be disturbed. . . . I will also give you rest from all your enemies. The LORD declares to you that the LORD himself will establish a house for you." (2 Sam. 7:9–11)

If you pay attention, you will notice that God flipped the focus of attention from what David wanted to do for God to what God had already done for David and to what God would continue to do for David's dynasty. God promised to build David's house.

The Hebrew word for house, *beit*, has different connotations. It can be the *building* structure in which a family lives, but it can also connote the *people* who constitute the family. David proposed to build a house, or building, for God, but God responded that he would build a house, or dynasty, for David. One of David's descendants would build the temple building.

> "He is the one who will build a house for my Name, and I will establish the throne of his kingdom forever. I will be his father, and he will be my son." (2 Sam. 7:13–14)

Did you catch the father-son language here? God established a covenant with David and promised to be faithful to David's descendants.

David's son Solomon inherited the kingdom when David died. The economy boomed as Solomon made lucrative trade agreements with the surrounding nations, and he built the temple in Jerusalem that David dreamed of constructing. The building was designed according to the same tripartite structure of the tabernacle, but much larger. The temple was a visual representation of what it meant for God to live in the midst of his people.

Solomon was the last king to rule over all twelve Israelite tribes. After his death, the kingdom split into two entities: the northern kingdom of Israel and the southern kingdom of Judah. To make matters more complicated, international empires that were stronger and more sophisticated than the Israelites were expanding and becoming a growing threat. To protect their kingdoms, many of the Israelite kings prioritized economic viability and political prowess over God's teachings.

Things Fall Apart

Even before the rise of the monarchy, prophets were an essential part of Israelite life. The early prophets—such as Nathan, Elijah, and Elisha—lived in the heyday of the Israelite kingdom. Their teachings are interwoven into the historical books that document the events of the kingdom (Samuel–Kings). They functioned as the mouthpiece of God to both the kings and the Israelite people. Prophets played in integral part in interpreting the law for the ever-changing Israelite society. They reminded the people of God's character, God's promises, and God's faithfulness, and they urged the people to live in alignment with the covenant.

The latter prophets, who have books named after them (Isaiah–Malachi), lived within the context of international empires that threatened the existence of God's people. The prophets repeatedly called the kings and the people to repent and to remember that survival did not depend on strategic, economic plans but on remaining faithful to God. These prophets were doing practical theology! They interpreted God's laws for the ever-changing Israelite context. They critiqued their own culture from within. They opposed the status quo and often suffered the consequences.

Many of the prophetic books followed a common tripartite message: *repent* before God, *return* to God, and God will *restore* his people. They used visual (and often graphic) language to probe, encourage, and rebuke the people. Sometimes the people responded, but apathy waited around every corner. The prophetic books showcase how God patiently pursued his people for hundreds of years. But a time came when punishment was inescapable and the prophets' messages changed. God's patience changed into determination to hold his people accountable for their choices. But even in the prophets' most dire messages, there was always a small glimmer of hope. God would never abandon the people. A remnant would survive the punishment, and through them God would restore his people through another exodus-like event.

In 721 BCE, when the Assyrian Empire demolished the northern kingdom of Israel, some Israelites fled to the southern kingdom of Judah. The Assyrians removed other Israelites from their homeland and replaced them with foreign people. The southern kingdom of Judah remained independent for slightly over one hundred years.

On the international scene, however, a new kingdom was gaining dominance. Babylon soon toppled Assyria from its height of power and made its way south toward Egypt. The small kingdom in the Judean hills, however, was in the way and uncooperative; and by 586 BCE, Babylon had completely destroyed the Southern Kingdom. The residents were then exiled and scattered throughout the Babylonian Empire. Those refugees from Judah were called *Judeans* in captivity. This name stuck and is where the term "Jew" originated. In fact, when we get to the Greek New Testament writings, *Judean* and *Jew* are the same word. We will discuss the significance of this later, but for now, it is good to know that the Babylonian exile marks the correct time to switch the name of God's people from *Israelite* to *Jew*. When the Babylonians destroyed the four-hundred-year-old temple built by Solomon, this marked the end of Israelite history that we call the First Temple Period.

The Trauma of Exile

The Israelites had formed their identity around being God's people, redeemed from slavery and given a land in which to be rooted. Now they were forcibly removed from their land—from the place that held the memory of how God had been present throughout their history. Understandably, being disconnected from their land was deeply traumatic and shook the people to the core. They were now ruled by a foreign entity and submerged in different cultural and religious norms. They no longer had a temple to orient them to their ancestral beliefs. Fortunately, they had some of their scrolls with historic writings, copies of hymns, and collections of wisdom literature. The pain of exile birthed the editing and organizing of their sacred scrolls that told their story.

Pause for a moment to consider the following question: What happens to your identity when you believe you were forged in the furnace of oppression and given a land of inheritance but are then uprooted from the land? What do you tell your children? How do you express your identity without the land? What happens when you are no longer a people united around worship at the temple in Jerusalem? Do you give up? How do you hold any hope? Deuteronomy had cast a vision for life in the land with harmonious relationships between people, God, and nature, but what happens when you are exiled from the place where God dwelt among you?

Questions like these prompted the Jews in exile to assemble and discuss their history, beliefs, and what went wrong in the past to result in their present situation. Scholars generally agree that synagogues began during this time and evolved over the next few centuries, when Jews prioritized meeting together to study and worship (cf. Ezek. 8:1; 14:1; 20:1). The word *synagogue* refers not to a building but to an assembly of people. Having been without a temple for two generations, the concept of worship shifted from temple sacrifices to Torah-centric study as a community.

People found solace in their sacred texts. Did not the prophets promise that if the people repented and returned to God, he would restore them? Was it too late to hope for restoration to happen? Israelite history revealed a pattern. In each major epoch, God had raised up a leader to bring about his purposes: the patriarchal period led by Abraham, the exodus period led by Moses, and the monarchy period led by David. The prophets identified the pattern that showed that God persistently pursued his people. God was faithful to every covenant, so he would be faithful to the Davidic covenant as well. The people could find hope in the fact that God was *Immanuel*—God with us. Based on the patterns of the past, the people placed hope in

God to lift up a leader, bring about deliverance, and usher his people into a new epoch of history.

Think of how enticing it may have been for people to read collectively the prophetic literature that painted an eschatological picture of a restored Jerusalem, their most significant city, and a restored temple that was a symbol of God's presence among them (Ezek. 37:28). How encouraging it must have been for this once-again oppressed people to mull over the idea that their capital city would be elevated higher than the mountains (metaphorically) and that God's incomparable power would be obvious to all peoples. The nations that had dominated them would be the same nations to travel to the glorious city of Jerusalem to worship God. It was a revolutionary idea to think that God alone would be king and that all other international empires would pale in comparison.

A New Beginning

On the international scene, Persia dominated Babylon and the Persian king, Cyrus the Great, initiated a different policy toward the conquered people in his territory. He granted permission to captives to return to their ancestral lands and build temples to worship their gods. Jews, who had only heard about their homeland from the older generations, had a choice: Did they want to return to Judea, or remain integrated in the communities where they had created new lives?

Initially, only a small percentage of Jews chose to return to Jerusalem. Joshua and Zerubbabel were the political and religious leaders who returned with the first wave of people. Then Ezra and Nehemiah brought another wave of people. Slowly, the Jews rebuilt their community and, most importantly, their temple. But the monetary funds from a small group of people were not enough to finance the type of city and temple that would be grand enough to live up to their eschatological hope. Think of the deep disappointment felt by those who saw the realistic view of their small temple in a small city (Hag. 2:3).

The Old Testament narrative ends with a small portion of Jews returning to the land. They rebuilt the temple and waited for God's glory to fill it (as they did for both the tabernacle and temple in Exod. 40 and 1 Kings 8). They learned from their recent history to avoid any of the sinful behaviors that had led to their seventy years in exile. There were no political boundaries to separate the Jews from other people since all of the land belonged now to Persia. Instead, the Jews began to establish social boundaries that identified them and separated them out as God's people. They zealously renewed their commitment to study and obey the Torah (Ezra 7:6, 10). They sent away their foreign spouses, strictly observed the law, kept kosher, and carefully followed the prohibition against work on the Sabbath.

The land, however, was not empty when the Jews returned. Remember how the northern kingdom of Israel was demolished by Assyria and the inhabitants replaced with foreigners? Some of those people had adopted Israelite beliefs—or something similar to Israelite beliefs (2 Kings 17:24–41). They had remained in the land while the Israelite inhabitants of the kingdom of Judah scattered throughout the Babylonian Empire. The people who had remained in the hill country were in the district ruled by the governor of Samaria and were known as the Samaritans. Complications ensued when Judeans returned from exile and claimed to be the true remnant of God's people. The Samaritans made similar claims and added that they had never left the land. Understandably, a certain amount of animosity developed specifically around the rebuilding of the temple in Jerusalem (Ezra 4–6; Neh. 2:10–20; 4:1–15), and the seeds of hatred grew between the Samaritans and the Jews until it reached a climax during the days of Jesus.

The conclusion of the Old Testament, though, should not be associated with an end of the development of Jewish thought and practice. The prophets looked at Torah and reinterpreted it for their day. The same tradition continued into the exile and beyond. The Jews were in an evolving religious civilization. The patriarchal way of life was different from the time of the monarchy, and the monarchy was very different from the exilic and postexilic times.[10] We would be amiss to try to monochrome the Israelites, or even Israelite beliefs, through the Hebrew Bible.

Hope for Restoration

One question remained: God promised restoration, but what would it look like? How many people had to return to the ancestral land to be confident that the restoration happened? Would God restore a kingdom like the one under David? What would happen to the Persian Empire? The Jews longed for the Messiah through whom God would deliver the people from the oppressive powers. One who would be like David—the king from a small village of Bethlehem who became great because he followed God's instructions. People believed that the Messiah would rebuild the Davidic kingdom and usher the Jews into a new era of renewal and restoration. Who but a descendant of David could unite the people under one rule, restore national sovereignty, build a proper temple, and bring back the glory days of prosperity?

Additionally, texts like Jeremiah 31:31–33 (cf. Deut. 30:6) spoke of a new covenant. Similar to those with Noah, Abraham, Moses, and David, this covenant would create kinship between God and humans. It would also imbed the instructions of God on the hearts of his people to transform their nature.

There were roughly six hundred years from early Israelite nationality to the Persian Empire. We should therefore expect to see a lot of cultural change, even *within* the Hebrew Scriptures, because of the length of time recorded. There were roughly another five hundred years between the rise of the Persian Empire and the time of Jesus. That is the same amount of time between William Shakespeare and the present. And think of the changes in culture, language, and international politics that have happened since Shakespeare! Likewise, we should expect to see an enormous amount of change within the thought, practice, religion, and culture of the Jews from the exile to the time of Jesus. These changes will be the subject of following chapters, but it is essential to remember that along with the changes there was also continuity with the ancient Israelite narrative preserved in their sacred texts. The Judaism of the New Testament time was fully rooted in Hebrew Scripture but had evolved to fit their modern context.

Jesus was not an outsider who appeared out of the blue to revolutionize the world. He fit into a developing story with which the Jewish community was familiar. The Scripture-soaked minds of the first-century Jews interpreted every single action and teaching of Jesus through the rich lens of Israelite history and texts. The original audience of Matthew's Gospel would have read the genealogy at the beginning of the book as an explanation of how Jesus belonged to the Israelite story. When readers saw the first words of the Gospel of John, "In the beginning," they would have realized that John was telling a Genesis-like narrative—a recreation story. John also described Jesus as the one who came to "tabernacle" (sometimes translated "dwell") among the people, suggesting to the reader that Jesus was Immanuel—God with us. The Gospel writers assumed their readers were familiar with the Old Testament text, people, and themes. As Christopher Wright declares, "The more you understand the Old Testament, the closer you will come to the heart of Jesus."[11]

2

LAND OF THE GOSPELS

People in the Bible were a land-oriented people. Their geography had a dramatic influence on their lives. In our modern, global society, we do not often pay attention to the specifics of our environment. When I ask people if their grocery store is uphill or downhill from their home, they rarely know the answer unless they walk the route. Vehicles, machines, and technology separate us from the effects of nature. We illuminate dark spaces and control air temperatures. Stores import food that is neither local nor seasonal. Modernization allows us to control our environment, which tends to remove us from our context. I am not arguing that modernization is bad; I simply want to bring awareness to how we remove ourselves from the influence of our environment, which was not the case in the ancient world.

Ignoring our context, however, does not mean we are immune to the influence of the natural world. Imagine if I showed you a picture of a long sandy beach with ocean waves crashing into the shore and the sun setting over the western horizon. We can look at the environment and make broad assumptions about the food, clothing, and activities in which people in that environment engage. Seafood is probably on local menus. Warm weather clothing and beachwear are likely the norm. The rhythm of life matches the scenery. Now imagine a second picture of a dramatic valley snaking through rugged mountain peaks. Snow is on the crestline and evergreens cling to the sheer rock faces. My guess is that we would make different assumptions about the food, clothing, and activities of those residents from the ones who live on the coast. Food might be gamier. Clothing must be rugged. The weather demands that building designs change to accommodate natural forces. Travel is more difficult and thus fewer tourists visit.

If these geographical influences affect our lives now with all of our modern technological advances, how much more so for those living off the land? Geography surrounded the people in the Bible and determined their food options, vocations, and openness to new ideas. Therefore, one aspect of understanding the Gospels is engaging the *places* of the Gospels.

The Big Picture: Introduction to the Land

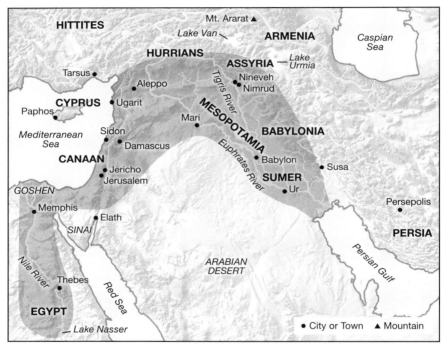

Figure 1. Fertile Crescent.

The area of land we call the Fertile Crescent begins in the north at the shoreline of the Persian Gulf and follows the Tigris and Euphrates northwest, almost to the Mediterranean Sea. The crescent bends along the eastern shoreline of the Mediterranean and ends at the southern end of the Nile River. The inhabitable land in the middle of the crescent is restricted by the expanse of the Arabian desert to the east and the Mediterranean Sea to the west. However, to the north and to the south are resource-rich lands that include powerful rivers. Mesopotamia had the Tigris and the Euphrates, and Egypt had the Nile. Each year, these rivers flooded and deposited mineral-rich soil on their banks, creating ideal agriculture zones.

The rivers also connected communities. If one region harvested an abundance of wheat, people constructed a raft or walked along the river bank to a neighboring community to trade their excess goods. Over time, communities pooled resources, shared goods, developed governments, organized armies, and conquered surrounding lands. Of course, such an explanation is overly simplified, but it illustrates with broad brush strokes how geography influenced the inhabitants of the riverine communities. The lands of Mesopotamia and Egypt became the birthplace of some of the most powerful empires of the ancient world: Egypt, Assyria, Babylon, and Persia.

In the middle of the Fertile Crescent—sandwiched between the sea in the west and the desert in the east, and between the northern and southern riverine lands—was a narrow band of inhabitable land. This was where most of the biblical narrative took place. This mountainous strip of land lacked the benefit of a powerful river. Of course, the Jordan River ran through a small portion of the land, and that small river did flood every year. However, the Jordan River was deep inside the crevice of the Rift Valley, and since its waters did not flow uphill to where the majority of people lived, this river did not provide the same benefits as the great rivers to the north and south. Rather, this land relied on precipitation for all of its water, and therefore the people in the land paid close attention to when and how much it rained. For those who did not live near a fresh-water spring, collecting rainwater to drink during the dry season was a necessary part of life.

The land of the Bible contained tall mountains and deep valleys. The rough texture of the land meant that the area was filled with small and diverse ecosystems that influenced development in unique ways. People were sensitive to the health of their land, since they lived in a fragile ecological area. Cities and villages were in close proximity to one another, but if they were located in dissimilar ecosystems, people's lifestyles were completely different. The bend and folds of the mountainous terrain created difficult obstacles for travelers to overcome. Connecting with *those* people over *that* ridge who are out of sight and, therefore, slightly less trustworthy, was problematic. This land between sea and desert was a fragmented terrain with unequal development that supported diverse populations that were difficult to unify under one government.

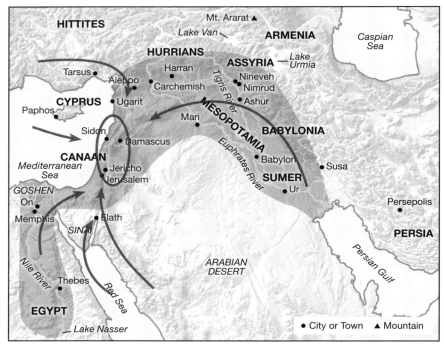

Figure 2. Primary Trade Routes of the Fertile Crescent.

While this land did not have the significant food, animal, and mineral resources that its riverine neighbors to the north and south had, it did have one valuable commodity—the roads. International trade routes ran through the narrow inhabitable piece of land. If any of the large, international empires wanted to trade goods or make war against each other, they had to travel on these roads. The land of the Bible was therefore a land bridge connecting Egypt to Mesopotamia and the desert with the sea.

At a glance, this land seems counterintuitive as the place of promise for God's people. The Old Testament describes the land as a place where the Israelites learned to depend on God just as the land depended on God (Deut. 11:11–15). The place did not have the capacity to support a world-dominating empire, so the Israelites were never equipped to conquer the world. However, even the greatest empires had to pass through Israelite terrain. If God's people lived according to their covenant, then they would be an example to the surrounding empires of what God's love, justice, and righteousness were like (Deut. 4:6). In other words, the land was not meant to be home to a world-*dominating* empire but instead home to a world-*influencing* people.

Agriculture and Religion

Two concepts of place are foundational to this conversation. The first one we noticed above: *Place influences how people live.* People in arid climates necessarily cultivate foods different from those in tropical climates, and it is the same for clothing and building materials. People tucked away in mountainous communities participate in activities different from those who live near the ocean. Terrain affects the mode and ease of travel and therefore the flow of information and access to new ideas. While modern technology erases some geographical obstacles, the lives of people in the Bible were tightly interwoven with their physical environment. Knowing where their cities were and what the geographical environment was like helps modern readers identify with the humanity of the people in the text.

Second, *place preserves memory.* Have you ever been in a location for the first time in years and walked across a particular spot on the pavement, only to have a previously forgotten memory spring to the forefront of you mind? This physical location triggered your memory. Think about the trauma of the Babylonian exile. The people who returned to Jerusalem came with only the stories the older generations had told them, but they had no experience of the place themselves. The memory of these stories, however, was preserved in the landscape. As they became reconnected to the land, the stories of their past pushed into their present. In the time of Jesus, the Jews lived in a land soaked with memories of their Israelite past. Mentioning a place name had the power to evoke the entire narrative of events that happened there. The authors and audiences of the biblical text shared the assumed knowledge of the living memory of their past. In our modern context—separated from the ancient land of the Israelites—we have to work harder to be cognizant of these connections, which is why this chapter is necessary.

People's lives were interwoven into the natural cycles of the land. People did not think of calendars as a linear measure of time but as cyclical—repeating itself. In our modern world, we begin a new year on the first of January, but those living in the land of the Bible began their year in September or October when the early, gentle rains marked the end of the dry season and the beginning of the rainy season. The early rains softened the ground and allowed farmers to break through the hard crust of earth with their plows. Farmers tended their soil and sowed their seeds before the

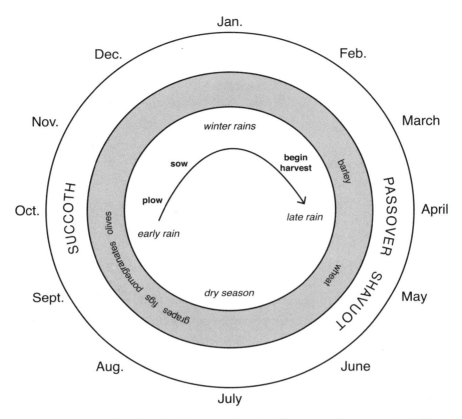

Figure 3. Agricultural and Religious Calendar (illustration by Drew McCall).

heavy rains arrived in December through February. By March, the first of the crops was ready. Farmers harvested barley in March and then wheat in April and May. By the end of the grain harvests, the rainy season stopped completely and the dry season began. The summer heat pushed the rest of the produce to fruition. Farmers harvested grapes, figs, and pomegranates in July through September, and they concluded the year's harvest by collecting olives in October. By then, the ground was baked hard by the summer sun, and farmers hoped that God would bring the early rains that would initiate the next agricultural cycle.

The Israelite religious calendar corresponded to the cyclical life of the land. The Israelites connected their national narrative, which recalled God's powerful acts in history, to the agricultural calendar. Ever year as the land progressed through its natural cycles, the Israelites remembered their identity as God's people. The beginning of the barley harvest marked the time of Passover and the memory of God's power to bring his people out of oppression in Egypt. The conclusion of the wheat harvest signaled a time to celebrate Shavuot and the memory of receiving the Torah at Mount Sinai. The completion of the year's olive harvest reminded them that God provided for the Israelites during their wilderness wanderings. Every year, the activities of normal life, as dictated by the natural cycle of the land, reminded the whole community of their national history and their identity as God's people.

The Gospel writers therefore assumed that their audience understood this agricultural and religious calendar. Take, for instance, two examples from the Gospel of John. In John 6:3–13, he describes the miracle of the multiplication of the loaves and the fish. We are told that the festival of Passover was approaching. Based on the information given above, we can deduce the timing of the event—around March or April when the barley harvest was complete. Therefore, it is no surprise in the narrative when the young boy showed up with barley loaves in his lunch (v. 9), because barley was the only grain available for bread that early in the year. April marked the final weeks of the rainy season—a time when colorful wildflowers covered the hills filled and "there was plenty of grass in that place" (v. 10). During Passover, people were mindful of the exodus from Egypt and the time in the wilderness where God provided manna for the Israelites.

In this chapter, we read that Jesus fed the hungry crowd by miraculously multiplying barley loaves and fish. Everyone ate their fill and yet twelve baskets of food were left over (possibly recalling the twelve tribes in the wilderness). Everything about the events in John seem to reembody the exodus narrative. Jesus' audience would not miss the parallels. They followed him the next day and asked for additional signs and wonders, stating, "Our ancestors ate the manna in the wilderness" (v. 31). They linked their personal experience in the present to the memory of their ancestors' experience in the past. The way John tells the story, Jesus was in the role of God by providing food for the people, even in a desolate situation. Jesus responded to the crowd's requests with a teaching about how he himself is the bread of life given by the Father to give life to the world (vv. 32–40).

A second example is found in John 7.[1] The beginning of the chapter states that the Feast of Succoth was near, which implies that the annual harvest was completed. Succoth was in late September or October, which implies the end of the dry season and the lack of stored water. People were anxious for the early rains that were necessary for the next agricultural cycle to begin, and this celebration of the completed harvest heightened their recognition of their reliance on God to provide rain. Just as God sustained their ancestors in the wilderness, the people needed God to provide rains for their survival. The weeklong harvest festival reminded them that God provided for their ancestors in the distant past (supplies in the wilderness), and he provided for the current generation in the recent past (harvest). They were therefore encouraged to have faith that God would provide once again for his people in the near future.

The Gospel of John says that Jesus missed the beginning of the Succoth festival in Jerusalem but arrived before the completion of the celebration. John 7:37 states that on the last day of the feast, the day in which people prayed for the beginning of the early rains, Jesus stood up to teach to the crowds. He began by saying, "Let anyone who is thirsty . . ." Think about that for a moment. It was October. Everyone was thirsty. Their stores of water were almost empty. They had just endured five months of the hot, desiccating sun, and they needed God to bring the early rains. Jesus continued, "On the last and greatest day of the festival, Jesus stood and said in a loud voice, 'Let anyone who is thirsty come to me and drink. Whoever believes in me, as Scripture has said, rivers of living water will flow from within them'" (vv. 37–38). On the final day of the festival when people were physically thirsty and praying that God would provide the necessary rains, Jesus claimed that he himself provided living water! Without stating it explicitly, Jesus put himself in God's position— the only source of water.

These are only two of many examples of how understanding the connection between the agricultural cycle of the land and the Jewish religious calendar illuminates the context of the Gospel stories. But what about the dramatic folds of the hills or the open valleys as discussed at the beginning of the chapter? How did geography influence the people and events of the Gospels? To answer these questions, we will compare three places that were significant in the life of Jesus: Nazareth, the place of his childhood; Capernaum, his home base during his public ministry; and Jerusalem, the place of the temple.

Lessons from Geography: Nazareth

Nazareth was a tiny village located in a south-facing, chalky basin on a low ridge in Galilee. The soil around Nazareth was of poor quality and water was scarce, so the land could support only a small community, and laborers most likely went to surrounding towns and cities to find work. From the village, residents looked down into the large, flat Jezreel Valley that contained major east–west roads. People in Nazareth had a certain amount of confidence that although the traders, pilgrims, and Roman soldiers passed on the roads below, they were unlikely to climb the slope of the hill to get to Nazareth unless they had a good reason to do so. While their community was not quite isolated, it was protected from an abundance of outside influences.

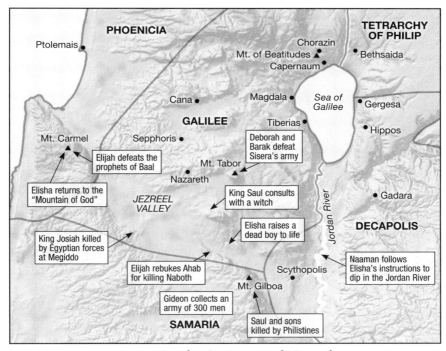

Figure 4. Israelite Stories around Nazareth.

Even though Nazareth was not built on a site to preserve ancient Israelite memories, the vantage point from the low ridge granted the residents a commanding view of the landscape on which many Israelite events occurred. And remember, place preserves memory. Several moments from Israelite history were embedded in the horizon. To the southwest are the high hills of Mount Carmel, where Elijah confronted the prophets of Baal (1 Kings 18); and across the Jezreel Valley sits the remains of the ancient city of Megiddo, where King Josiah died when he attempted to interfere in international politics (2 Kings 23). At the base of Mount Gilboa, located to the southeast, Gideon gathered a ragtag group of soldiers to fight a battle for freedom (Judg. 7). And on its top, the Philistines killed King Saul and his sons (1 Sam. 31). Nearby is the Hill of Moreh with the ancient town of Shunem at its base, where a woman provided a guest room for Elisha (2 Kings 4). To the east of Nazareth sits the round hill of Mount Tabor, which is where the Israelite forces of Deborah and Barak battled against Sisera (Judg. 4–5). From tales of the judges to those of prophets and kings, a grand Israelite narrative is preserved in the landscape around Nazareth. Although little is known about Jesus' childhood, it is easy to imagine him climbing the rocks on the edge of the village with his parents and talking about their heritage as God's people, seeing the landscape through their preserved memories.

Lessons from Geography: Capernaum

When Jesus entered his public ministry, he moved his home base from Nazareth's semi-isolated environment to Capernaum, a town built along the northern shoreline of the Sea of Galilee. Along its flat shoreline ran a major trade route that facilitated the exchange of goods, its freshwater lake teemed with fish, and its soil was ideal for agriculture. Therefore, Capernaum grew into a large town populated with fishermen, farmers, skilled craftsmen, Roman soldiers, tax collectors, and synagogue officials. Among Capernaum's many neighbors were Jewish towns such as Magdala, Zealot towns such as Gamla, and Roman Decapolis cities such as Hippos.

Instead of Nazareth, then, Jesus chose Capernaum as his base of operation for his public ministry. The Gospel writers do not explain the strategy behind such a decision, but the geography suggests a few reasons. A bustling town like Capernaum was home to a variety of people accustomed to interacting with new ideas. Jesus' message of hope and of restoration, albeit based on the Israelite narrative, was a new interpretation of Scripture. Only a community accustomed to hearing new ideas with an open mind could listen with curiosity to Jesus' radical message. Additionally, Jesus discipled

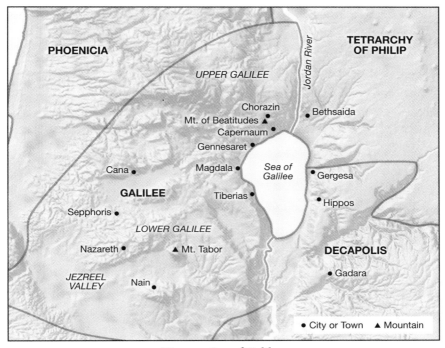

Figure 5. Sea of Galilee.

a group of twelve men to carry his ideas throughout the known world. Capernaum's location put Jesus and the disciples in a microcosm of the Roman world with peasants, scholars, traders, soldiers, zealots, and Roman citizens. Jesus did not need to travel far to demonstrate for his disciples how to interact with diverse populations. Such opportunities were never available in Nazareth.

Lessons from Geography: Jerusalem

Located high in the Judean hill country, Jerusalem was vastly different from both Nazareth and Capernaum. The bends and folds of the surrounding hills created a hemmed in and protected feel, which contributed to the population's suspicious attitude toward outsiders. Historically, the location of the city presented both challenges and benefits to its inhabitants. The hills kept invaders and foreign, cultural influences at bay, but they also hindered the inhabitants' access to wealth, trade, and exotic goods. People from Jerusalem had to travel a day's journey through difficult terrain to reach international roads.

In contrast to both Nazareth and Capernaum, the city of Jerusalem held layers of Israelite memory in its terrain. Most importantly, it was the location of the temple and home to the memory of their great leader King David. Jerusalem was the capital city of the southern kingdom of Judah, and it was the first city to be re-occupied by the Jews who returned from exile.

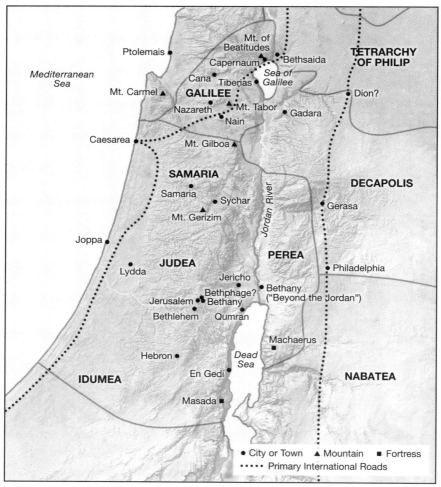

Figure 6. Jerusalem in the Judean Hill Country.

Due to the temple, Jerusalem was the religious focal point for the Jews. In the next chapter, we will talk about the complexity of the political and religious situation in Jerusalem during the time of the Gospels; but for now, we can think of the city as the ivory tower of Judaism. Although Jesus was often in Jerusalem, the inhabitants there were more reluctant to embrace his interpretations of Scripture than those in Capernaum.

Each of these three towns—the small village of Nazareth, the large town of Capernaum, and the robust metropolis of Jerusalem—played significant roles in the life to Jesus. The geography of each place contributed to people's lifestyles and openness to new ideas.

Conclusion

Even though we intuitively know that geography matters, we rarely spend time questioning its effects on people in the biblical narratives. Becoming familiar with the geography of the Bible helps modern readers understand the people of the Bible, providing information not explicitly discussed in the narratives—such as livelihood and access to roads and communication.

On almost every page of the Bible, we find geographical information. If we are curious enough, then we can learn new information about Jesus' world. What did the terrain look like? What time of year did events happen, and were those events connected to the religious calendar? And last, but not least, what memories of historical events are preserved in that landscape? The answers to these questions will break open the coded, assumed information shared between the original Gospel author and audience and allow us to enter into the vivid, multicolored, complex reality of Jesus.

Of course, the political geography of the time is another significant detail, but we will need to embark upon a history lesson before we can dive into the complexity of the political boundaries during Jesus' ministry.

3

INTERNATIONAL DRAMA

We concluded the Old Testament narrative in chapter 1 with a small group of Jews who returned to Judea and built a small temple. In this chapter, we pick up the storyline and take it to the time right before the birth of Jesus. Since we have hundreds of years of dramatic and world-altering international history to engage, we have our work cut out for us. At the same time, we need to keep an eye on the smaller group of Jews who were forced to adapt to the international shifts in culture. While I describe changes to Jewish thought and practice, Jews lived in different places and their unique contexts influenced their experienced reality, so I will prioritize my focus on the small group of Jews who returned from exile to the hills of Judea. But as I have said before, I am painting with broad brushstrokes with the intention of understanding the context Jesus lived in during the first century.

The history in this chapter may not sound familiar to you since it is not well known in Christian circles. The time period we are concerned with here is commonly brushed aside as "four hundred years of silence." Such a label dismisses the significance of this time period. The phrase came out of the assumption that since the Protestant version of the Old Testament ends with Malachi and the New Testament begins with Matthew, then no other writings from that time were inspired by God. They believe that the history "between" these books must not have been important and that God was silent during these years.

But God was not silent. When is God ever silent? If we examine other writings produced during this time period, we will see the growing development of the Jewish faith. Some of those writings are included in the Apocrypha, which some Christian traditions have inserted into their Bible between the Old and New Testament texts. If that is so with your Bible, some of the following history may then sound familiar to you. The specific conversation of how faith traditions chose which books to include as Scripture, much less how to order the books, is outside the scope of this project, albeit a fascinating topic you should explore at some point.[1]

The point I want to make here is that the phrase "four hundred years of silence" is a misnomer. God was not silent, and the Jewish community was not static. They went through huge, revolutionary changes. In this chapter, we will follow the drama that had a tremendous impact on the development of Jewish beliefs.

By necessity, we will alternate between a large overarching view of significant international players and the much smaller, although locally significant, Jewish leadership anchored primarily in Jerusalem. Do not forget the way the Old Testament narrative ends—with the hope that God was going to restore his people, even if they did not know what that looked like. We begin our dive into history with one of the greatest revolutionaries to change the political arena around the Mediterranean Sea: Alexander the Great.

Alexander the Great

Figure 7. Alexander mosaic c. 100 BCE, House of the Faun,
Pompeii (by unknown artist; public domain).

The primary international kingdoms in the narrative up to this point were the empires in the Fertile Crescent. Egypt, Assyria, Babylon, and Persia were prominent kingdoms on one another's horizon lines, and they either bartered goods and services or fought over trade routes. The political context, however, took a dramatic turn in the fourth century BCE with Alexander III of Macedonia. Alexander initially set out to the east from Macedonia to conquer the Persian Empire. In the end, Persia was too small of a goal. By the age of twenty-six, Alexander had continued his eastern campaign all the way to the Indus River and became the mightiest, wealthiest, and most celebrated warrior of that time.

Alexander had more in mind than conquering territory though: he wanted to transform the eastern "barbarian" cultures.[2] In the generation prior to Alexander, the famous Greek rhetorician Isocrates stated, "Our city [Athens] has so much surpassed the rest of mankind in thought and in speech that her students have become the teachers of the rest of the world."[3] Alexander's life embodied Isocrates' ideal. Alexander was a student of the Greek philosopher Aristotle and was fascinated by Greek poetry, thought, medicine, and polity. As Alexander expanded his empire, he administered it according to the Greek *polis* (city-state). His soldiers settled in the newly formed cities, married local women, and educated the population in Greek culture. They built temples to their gods, theaters to tell the stories of their gods, and gymnasiums in which to train the body to physical perfection and the mind in philosophical discussion.[4] As Isocrates explained, the name of the Greeks (Hellenes) no longer described a *race* of people but instead described a way of *thinking*.

Figure 8. Alexander the Great marble bust c. 100 BCE–100 CE
(Brooklyn Museum; Charles Edwin Wilbour Fund; public domain).

Alexander's career was exciting but short. Only six years after the fighting at the Indus River, Alexander died from malaria at the age of thirty-two. The early death of this charismatic leader and military genius created a leadership vacuum that was impossible to fill. In this vacuum, his generals carved up the empire among themselves and then proceeded to fight each other for the next forty years to enlarge their own dynasties.[5]

After decades of war, two generals—Ptolemy and Seleucus—emerged with the majority of what had been Alexander's empire. Ptolemy took the territory to the southeast of the Mediterranean, including Egypt. Seleucus took the territory to the northeast of the Mediterranean, encompassing lands as far east as the Persian Gulf. The land that had been Israelite territory prior to the Babylonian exile was precariously sandwiched between them.

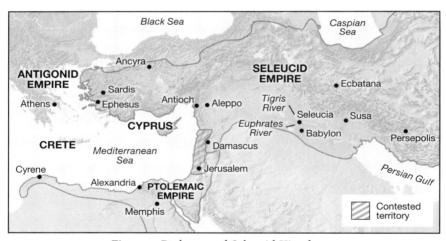

Figure 9. Ptolemy and Seleucid Kingdoms.

A Judean Focus

In the midst of the changing international landscape, the people living in Judea went on with their daily lives without needing to engage these struggles. Initially, the Ptolemies dominated the eastern seaboard of the Mediterranean; but in 201 BCE, the Seleucids successfully pushed them back toward Egypt. As these larger international fights continued, local people maintained a decent amount of autonomy as long as they paid taxes to the ruling party. The Jews living in Judea were allowed to worship as they preferred. In effect, the people could duck their heads and live their lives without bothering too much with these struggles. Even when the center of political power shifted from the Ptolemies in Egypt to the Seleucids in Mesopotamia, the religious focus of those in Judea never shifted away from the temple in Jerusalem.

Even with such autonomy, life for the Jews was complicated. To the north of Judea, the Samaritans embraced the changes Hellenism offered. They built huge cities patterned on the Greek polis and opened their arms to new trade. Significantly, Alexander the Great gave the Samaritans permission to build a large temple on Mount Gerizim to rival the Jewish temple in Jerusalem.

The Jews, however, were not unified in how to preserve their culture against the influences of Hellenism. As Greek language and customs took root, people created new, lucrative, international connections, but only by adopting Hellenism. Some learned the Greek language for trade purposes, and others gave Greek names to their children. Hellenism did not eradicate local cultures but rather blended Greek culture with other cultures.[6] The Jews debated how much of the Greek way of life was adaptable and how much needed to be rejected. Speaking Greek was acceptable, because it opened channels of communication and trade across a vast network; but should Greek forms of entertainment in the theaters or Greek education in the gymnasiums be permitted? For the Jews at that time, the debate centered on how much of Hellenism could be embraced before they betrayed their Jewish identity. When did accommodation become apostasy?

The infiltration of Hellenism therefore forced a conversation about what constituted Jewish identity apart from political borders. They did not control their ancestral land with a Davidic-style kingdom, so what identified the Jews as God's people? Four nonnegotiable Jewish practices emerged as key ethnic identifiers. These are worth memorizing, because Jesus was often drawn into debates around these topics. When these issues come up in conversations in the Gospels, remember their deep roots and how interwoven they became with Jewish identity. When the leaders of the people became upset with Jesus, it was not always because he had a different opinion, but because they were not sure if Jesus was pushing the boundaries too far. The four nonnegotiables the Jewish community established that identified them as God's people were the kosher dietary laws, circumcision, worship at the one temple in Jerusalem, and adherence to the biblical festivals (including the Sabbath).[7] Although these practices were observed by all Jewish communities, the specifics of *how* to observe these identifiers were flexible and determined by each local community.

The reality of how the temple priests used their positions in the temple became particularly tricky. Ideas of a grand temple in an elevated city to which all the empires of the earth came to worship God had been part of the picture the Jews imagined for when God vindicated his people. The temple was central to the identity of the Jews, who worshiped only one God. The reality was that the one who controlled the temple had enormous power, wealth, and prestige. Mixing the ideal symbol of the temple with the power associated with it and the influence Hellenism brought created problems that persisted until the final destruction of the temple in 70 CE. But I get ahead of myself.

Jason was a priest from the line of Zadok and thus considered a true Levitical priest. He believed, however, that Hellenism was a positive way to reform and grow the influence of Judea. Remember how Alexander's generals fought for portions of his empire? Well, the Seleucids were based in Mesopotamia and since 201 BCE were in control of the Judean Hills. Jason sent a sizable tribute to the Seleucid ruler, with promises of more, in exchange for the title of high priest for himself. Jason promised the Seleucids that he would use his position to further the growth of Hellenism by bringing theaters, colosseums, and hippodromes to Jerusalem. Unlike other urban areas throughout Seleucid territory, Jews were the majority in Jerusalem, which they had not only built but administered as well. And now Jason was at the helm of turning Jerusalem into the most important Hellenized city for the Jews.

A few years later, Jason's rival, Menelaus, sent an even larger tribute to the Seleucid king with hope of supplanting Jason as high priest. Understandably, the people were not happy with Jason for using temple money to buy his position, but at least Jason was from the priestly line of Zadok. Although Menelaus had no such claims, money speaks volumes, and the Seleucids granted Menelaus the position. Perceived corruption and bribery in the priesthood infuriated some Jews, who concluded that the sacred temple was becoming a place of corruption.

International Drama Continues

On the international scene, the struggle for power persisted as the Seleucid Empire continued to chip away at the Ptolemaic Empire to the south. Simultaneously, the Parthian Empire became a growing threat on the Seleucid's eastern frontier and, to the far west, the dangerous and dark storm cloud of the Roman Republic was taking shape. The Seleucids soon found themselves fighting battles on all sides, wearing themselves thin, and draining their coffers.

Figure 10. Antiochus IV bust (Altes Museum, Berlin; public domain).

Political pressure came to a head during the reign of Antiochus IV Epiphanes (*epiphanes* means "the manifest God"—a title Antiochus IV granted to himself). Antiochus IV inherited a broken kingdom of internal strife and financial struggles. Since wars were expensive, to compensate for the kingdom hemorrhaging funds, Antiochus increased the taxes of all subjected peoples. Naturally, tempers ran short and the people began to hate Antiochus for his oppressive rule. Polybius, a historian in the days of Antiochus, said that the ruler was not "epiphanes" ("God Manifest") but "epimanes" ("crazy").[8] Then Antiochus minted coins imprinted with the phrase, "Basileus Antiochus, God Manifest, Bearer of Victory." Did you catch that? The foreign power ruling Judea claimed to be God Manifest. The majority of the Jews soon had a growing animosity toward him, which only worsened when Menelaus the high priest plundered the temple in Jerusalem to meet his financial obligations to Antiochus. At this point, the people could no longer tolerate the corruption of the priesthood that served to finance Antiochus's military campaigns.

Figure 11. Antiochus IV Epiphanes coin with Greek inscription, "Antiochus, image of God, bearer of victory" (public domain).

A Judean Focus

While Antiochus, the "crazy one," was busy fighting the Ptolemies in Egypt, rumors began to circulate that he had died on the battlefield. Great rejoicing broke out in Jerusalem! They were free of the tyranny of the king. People in Judea took advantage of the situation and withheld the excessive taxation payments. Unfortunately, the rumors of Antiochus's death were false. The king was alive and furious at the blatant challenge to his authority.

When Antiochus retreated from the battlefront near Egypt, he stormed into the mountains of Judea and to the city of Jerusalem. His patience evaporated for the Jews and their special ways of separating themselves from the Hellenized population. Do you remember what the key identifiers were for the Jews? Well, Antiochus sought to eradicate them all. He slaughtered a pig on the altar, forced the priests to eat it, and then dedicated the temple to Zeus. He instructed his generals to burn copies of Torah scrolls, and he forbade the Jewish population from observing kosher laws. They, like the priests in the temple, were forced to eat pork. He forbade Jewish families from circumcising their sons, and if they did, the child was killed and hung around the mother's neck. Antiochus violently attacked each of the four nonnegotiables that established Jewish ethnicity. He wanted to force the people to give up their beliefs, traditions, and identity, but the Jews wanted to love God and remain his faithful covenant people.

These violent retaliatory actions of Antiochus forced the Jews into action. Seleucid generals traveled throughout the territories, and in each community, slaughtered a pig and forced the Jewish people to consume it. When the generals made their way to a modest city of Modi'in (west of Jerusalem and close to the coastal plain), a priestly family showed up for the pig slaughter. Instead of capitulating to the demands of the Seleucid generals, one priest took a spear and drove it into the general's body (an action reminiscent of the religious fervor of Phinehas in Num. 25:6–8). And so the Jewish revolt against the mighty Seleucid Empire began with this priest, Mattathias the Hasmonean, and his sons (1 Macc. 2:44–48; 3:5–6).

A Fight for Jewish Independence

As with many grassroot rebellions, the greatest challenge was convincing people of the need to confront a powerful enemy and then organizing those volunteers into a viable force of fighters. Mattathias needed to convince the Hasidim ("religious ones") to join the resistance, but that required the Hasidim to compromise their Sabbath observance practices. Remember, some Jews associated the punishment of the Babylonian exile with a failure to honor God and the Sabbath. The Hasidim were determined not to make the same mistake, even at the cost of their own lives. For this reason, the Seleucid soldiers quickly realized that battles were easier on the Sabbath, because the Hasidim would not resist. Mattathias, however, was able to persuade the Hasidim that fighting for their beliefs on the Sabbath was indeed a righteous act.

Even with the compliance of the Hasidim, Mattathias and his sons had a minuscule chance of success against the Seleucids. One factor, however, did work in favor of the small group of Jewish rebels: the Seleucids were fighting much larger wars on the international stage. With the Parthians on their eastern border and the Ptolemies on their southern border, the threat of Rome now loomed large on their western border. Although quelling the Jewish resistance was important, this small rebellion in the inconsequential territory of the Judean hills was not their highest priority. In addition to these external pressures, their internal leadership structure had begun crumbling. The Seleucid kingdom now had too many fractures in its own ranks and was splitting apart under the pressure of competing interests. All of this led to success for this ragtag Jewish offensive.

The book of 2 Maccabees recounts the triumphant stories of Mattathias and his sons leading a band of rebels against a strong international power as if they were David against Goliath. Indeed, they were the small, inexperienced, poorly equipped group of resisters going up against a large, military machine. They credited God's favor for their success. The rebels fought persistently and with righteous indignation, believing God to be on their side. You should hear faint messianic undertones here: the Hasmonean family, which later became known as the Hasmonean Dynasty, saw themselves in the role of the shepherd king.

When Mattathias died, leadership passed to his son Judas Maccabeus ("the hammer"), who continued fighting against the Seleucids. For three years, the rebels fought their way into the heart of Judea to wrestle Jerusalem out of the hands of the enemy. In one glorious victory, they freed Jerusalem and the temple from pagan hands.

The small Jewish rebellion succeeded against the Seleucids, because they pushed against the weakened, hairline fractures of a crumbling kingdom. The fervor of the Jewish revolutionists burned hotter than Antiochus IV's determination to force the Jews to accommodate Hellenism, so he finally lifted the prohibitions against the unique Jewish practices that set them apart from Hellenism.

On the twenty-fifth day of Chislev (roughly December), on the same day when three years earlier Antiochus IV Epiphanes defamed the temple by slaughtering a pig on the altar, Judas Maccabeus led the people in a victorious celebration to rededicate the temple to God. Despite lacking the necessary amount of oil required to keep the lamps burning during the temple purification process, the lamps miraculously stayed lit and God's house was cleansed. This event was woven into the religious calendar and celebrated annually as the Feast of Dedication, or Hanukkah (cf. John 10:22).

For eight days, the people partied. During the previous three years of Seleucid rule, the Jews had been prohibited from celebrating any of their festivals, so on this occasion, they borrowed the symbols from Succoth, which was the holiday that honored God's provision in the wilderness—a time when though the Israelites had nothing, they lacked nothing, because God was faithful. While the Jews rededicated the temple, people gathered ivy-wreathed sticks, beautiful branches, and palm fronds, and they sang songs of thanksgiving (2 Macc. 10:5–9). In this way, they celebrated Succoth along with their newfound freedom from their oppressor. The Jews had successfully fought for freedom. During these eight days, the symbols of Succoth became intertwined with the celebration of independence and the festival took on nationalistic overtones.

Take a moment to think about the details in this story. The Jews liberated Jerusalem from oppressive Hellenistic occupiers, regained religious freedom, and rejoiced by singing hymns and waving palm branches. Does this scene sound familiar? Roughly one hundred years later, Jesus would enter a Roman-controlled Jerusalem with similar pomp and circumstance. In his day, the crowds would yearn once again for a dynamic leader to rally them against occupying forces. They flocked to Jesus and ushered him into the city, singing songs of independence and waving palm branches. When the Gospel writers record the events of Palm Sunday, they do not need to mention Judas Maccabeus and the celebration of Hanukkah. The crowd's actions were enough to echo the events of the prior century. We will discuss this within the context of Passion Week in a later chapter, but noting it here allows us to see how the historical background made Jesus' actions so shocking. Ushering a leader into the city, singing songs of independence, and waving palm branches was a dramatic and dangerous statement to make in front of Roman soldiers. In effect, the crowd was celebrating the arrival of the one who would bring liberation to the city.

High Priest and King?

Judas Maccabeus liberated Jerusalem, and the people rededicated the temple, but the position of high priest was not filled with a priest from the line of Zadok, and the resistance fighting was not over. After Judas died, two of his brothers, Jonathan and Simon, assumed the mantle of leadership and continued the military campaigns against the Seleucids for another two decades. Finally, under Simon's rule, the Seleucid king granted independence to the Jewish state for the first time since Judah's fall to Babylon in 586 BCE. As a sign of appreciation, the Jewish people gave Simon the title of high priest (1 Macc. 14:41), which meant that a military leader now held the highest position in the temple.

With the intensity of pushing back against a domineering empire gone and a high priest installed in the Jerusalem temple, the people enjoyed stability for the first time in years—which led to a debate among the Jews if this marked the fulfillment of God's restoration. After all, the Jews had a leader, a little patch of land, a temple, and independence.

After Simon's death, his son John Hyrcanus became the ruler of the small Jewish, territory. He wanted to expand his control to the edges of the ancient Israelite borders from the time of King David. The Hasidim participated in the early stages of the revolt but did not want to fight additional military battles. Expanding a kingdom was not the same as fighting for freedom. The Hasidim had helped to regain Jerusalem, the temple, and religious independence, but they did not support John Hyrcanus's expansionist campaign. Determined not to let his goal be thwarted, John Hyrcanus hired mercenaries to enhance his depleted volunteer army.

From Defense to Offense

The older generations gave their lives for independence, but the younger generation wanted more. John Hyrcanus managed to push the borders of his kingdom out of the confining hills of Judea to the edges of what had been King David's kingdom. He took advantage of the Seleucid's weakened control over the surrounding territory by going on the offense against powerfully fortified cities. After conquering the region of Idumea to the south of Judea, the army pushed north to the region of Samaria, where they destroyed the Samaritan temple on Mount Gerizim. The ruins of that temple were still visible when Jesus met the Samaritan woman at the well and she said, "Our ancestors worshiped on this mountain [Mount Gerizim], but you Jews claim that the place where we must worship is in Jerusalem" (John 4:20).

City after city fell in bloody battles led by John Hyrcanus. Conquered peoples were forced to become Jewish by circumcising their males—the only time forced conversion was a part of Jewish history. Within two generations, the Jewish fighting efforts morphed from resisting oppressive forces and protecting religious freedom, to becoming the aggressor and forcing a small (and painful!) demonstration of Jewish conversion.

As Jewish territory and freedom grew, Jews from the diaspora came to live in the expanding Jewish kingdom. This was likely the time when a small Jewish group decided to create a new village in Galilee called Nazareth. The name has links to the Hebrew word for "branch" (*netzer*), which may convey the villagers' messianic hope in the promised branch from the root of Jesse (Isa. 11:1; Jer. 23:5; 33:15; Zech. 3:8; 6:12). We cannot say for sure why they named the village Nazareth, but we can guess that they were among the waves of immigrants who witnessed Hyrcanus expand the Jewish kingdom and felt like they once again had a home.

John Hyrcanus heralded the immigrants' arrival as the hoped-for restoration from the Babylonian exile. The Hasmonean family overthrew the oppressive foreign rule, and they spearheaded the endeavors of expanding and beautifying the small temple that the original returnees had built in Jerusalem. First Maccabees describes the Hasmonean reign as nothing less than messianic.[9] The Hasmonean family was celebrated as the savior of Israel—the ones who brought deliverance. But not everyone agreed.

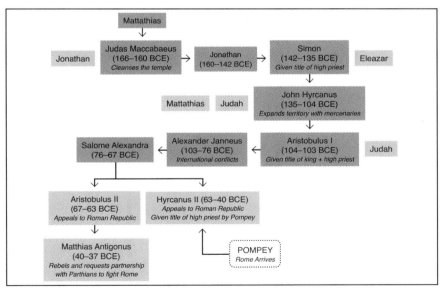

Figure 12. Hasmonean Ruling Dynasty (illustration by Drew McCall).

John Hyrcanus passed the Jewish kingdom, along with the role of high priest, to his son Aristobulus, who assumed the title of king. For the first time in Jewish history, the titles of king and high priest were held by the same person. And for the first time in Jerusalem, the one called king was not from the tribe of Judah nor the line of David. How do you think this went over with the people? As you may guess, they were of mixed opinion. What better choice did they have than to accept Aristobulus as high priest and king? After all, having a Jewish leader was better than having a foreign leader. But was *this* the restoration God had promised? Military holidays were turned into religious holidays. The high priesthood belonged to the ruling class of society, but they were not of the line of Zadok. The roles of king and high priest were combined. Conquered peoples from surrounding communities were forced to convert to Judaism. And the names of the members of the ruling class were becoming more Hellenized. Mattathias, Judas, Simeon—all good Jewish names; Hyrcanus and Aristobulus—all Hellenized names. While a name alone does not indicate a worldview, these names did reflect the influence Greek culture had on the small Jewish nation.

By the time Aristobulus's younger brother, Alexander Janneus, inherited the kingdom along with the titles of high priest and king, the Hasmonean family line had evolved. Mattathias had been the patriarch of the priestly family in Modi'in, but now the Hasmonean family had Alexander Janneus as the head of an increasingly Hellenized, powerful ruling family in Jerusalem.

From Independence to Occupation

Among themselves, the Jewish people reacted in different ways to the propagation of Hellenism in their society. Some held to a strict obedience to Torah (Pharisees). Some advocated for violent revolt (Zealots). Others chose to assimilate (Sadducees), while some chose escapism (Essenes). These sects will be discussed in greater detail in chapter 5, but mentioning them here helps us recognize that the people groups that show up in the Gospel accounts of Jesus' life did not simply represent different religious beliefs. Many Jews, regardless of the sect they identified with, believed that the well-being of the nation was connected to a whole-hearted return to their covenant with God. Each group developed out of generations of wrestling with and reacting to complex social and political developments. Each group came to different conclusions regarding God's promised restoration of the Jewish people.

This increasing complexity within Jewish society proved to be a challenge for the political leadership. As we have seen, Alexander Janneus ruled with the joint titles of high priest and king. In the cultural wars, Alexander Janneus's father and older brother sided with the Sadducees over against the Pharisees, because the Sadducees were more aware of the social and economic opportunities that arose with Hellenism. Janneus, too, favored Hellenism, which was a decision that brought him into direct conflict with the conservative Pharisees—a conflict that became so heated that at one time Janneus ordered over eight hundred Pharisees to be crucified!

Figure 13. Salome Alexandra coin (from *Promptuarii Iconum Insigniorum a Seculo Hominum* published by Guillaume Rouillé in Lyon in 1553; public domain).

Upon Alexander Janneus's death, his wife Salome Alexandra, also known as Shlomtzion (Peace of Zion), took the throne. Salome ruled in the final years of the independent Jewish kingdom (76–67 BCE). She was a pious ruler who honored the Torah and reigned with justice. Salome switched her alliance from the Sadducees to the previously maligned Pharisees—the group her husband had adamantly resisted. She held the title of queen, but due to her gender, she was not high priest. Salome appointed her Pharisee-sympathizing son, Hyrcanus II, to the priesthood in her stead.

During her reign, Salome successfully maintained a strong military and spearheaded a handful of campaigns and peacemaking efforts. She worked with Jewish leaders to guarantee a Torah education for boys and girls in every Jewish town.[10] She facilitated the introduction of the *ketubah*, a marriage contract created to protect women in marriage and divorce. She fought for the dignity of the common person. Her reign was as refreshing as a cold drink on a hot day, and many named their daughters after her.[11]

Unfortunately, peace did not last long. Before Salome's death, her two sons went to war against each other over the combined position of high priest and king. Each brother turned to different allies for support. Hyrcanus II gained the popular vote from the Pharisees, and Aristobulus II gained the money, army, and backing of the Sadducees.

This is where an outsider entered the Jewish conflict and created a name for himself. A man named Antipater sided with Hyrcanus II throughout the Hasmonean civil war. (You may know of Antipater's son, Herod the Great, but we will come to his role in this saga shortly.) Antipater was Idumean[12]—one of the people groups forced to convert to Judaism during John Hyrcanus's expansionistic campaigns. Antipater knew that the position of high priest was out of his reach because he was not Jewish, but he was an influential person of power in his role of administrator. Antipater took advantage of Hyrcanus's weak character and prodded Hyrcanus toward war, while simultaneously spreading suspicion about Aristobulus among the wealthy Jews.

Neither of Salome's sons gained an upper hand in their civil war, and each looked for powerful, international allies to back them. Hyrcanus and Aristobulus recognized the growing influence of the Roman Republic and sent emissaries to the west to ask the large, imperial force to put its weight behind him over his brother.

This narrative is shocking, right? Only six generations earlier, Mattathias was collecting a ragtag group of rebels to fight off an external imperial power; and now, due to internal power struggles, his descendants are inviting a foreign empire into the power vacuum. Rome, of course, was happy to respond. Gnaeus Pompeius Magnus—or Pompey the Great as he is known in English—was a respected political and military leader in the late Roman Republic. He fought military battles on the African continent, political battles in Rome, and maritime battles against pirates on the Mediterranean Sea. Rome responded to the pleas from Hyrcanus and Aristobulus by sending Pompey to Jerusalem. Local Jewish forces did not stand a chance against the Roman legions.

The Arrival of Rome

Figure 14. Gnaeus Pompeus Magnus (Pompey) marble bust, c. 1800s (Florence, Italy; on display in Chateau de Vaux-le-Vicomte, France; public domain).

In 63 BCE, when Pompey quelled the civil war in Jerusalem, he went into the temple—not to plunder the goods but to satisfy his curiosity about a temple that did not contain statues. Pompey touched nothing, and when he left, he gave orders to the priests in charge to cleanse the temple and rededicate it to the Jewish God. Even though Pompey acted honorably, his entrance into the Holy of Holies reminded the people that they were under foreign dominance again. Not even the temple, God's house, was secure.

Pompey granted Hyrcanus II the position of high priest and ostracized his brother Aristobulus, and Antipater was retained as governor.[13] The title of king was taken away from the Hasmonean family and now Rome was in charge.

While Antipater was familiar with Jewish life and practices, he did not share the same Jewish historical narrative of exile, return, and restoration. Rome knew of his unfaltering loyalty to Rome, which is why they chose him to rule as governor in Jerusalem. In fact, once Pompey brought Roman control in the land, it was Antipater—not Hyrcanus—who convinced the Jews to live happy and undisturbed lives by accepting Rome as their ruler instead of their bitter enemy.[14] Blatantly pursuing an ambitious political agenda. Antipater appointed his son Phasael as governor of Jerusalem and his son Herod as governor of Galilee. His family grabbed more and more political power.

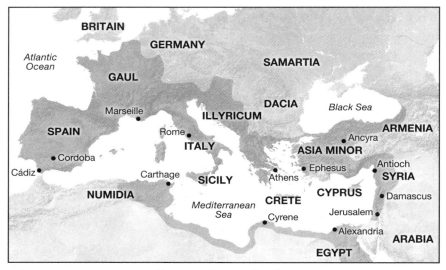

Figure 15. Roman Empire.

Although the Hasmonean Dynasty came to an end, they were not done resisting. Pompey stripped Aristobulus II of his royal position, but his son Antigonus continued the struggle for power. Since Antigonus could not fight Rome on his own, he looked to the Parthians in the east for assistance. The Parthians saw an opportunity to prevent Rome's eastern growth, and so they joined Antigonus in an attack against Judea.

Herod and Phasael were governors on behalf of Rome when the Parthians asked for a peace treaty. Herod suspected treachery and departed for Galilee. Phasael and Hyrcanus the high priest met with the Parthians and were taken captive and killed. Herod then fled to Rome for help. Rome understood the danger of the Parthians on their eastern border and the need for a loyal ruler in Judea, so they gave Herod the title of king of the Judeans and sent legions of Roman soldiers back with him to Jerusalem.

Concluding Thoughts

Alexander the Great ushered in the tidal wave of Hellenism that forced the Jews to grapple with issues regarding their foundational beliefs. They lacked land, political power, and armies, so what identified them as God's people? The three hundred years following Alexander were filled with intrigue, hidden agendas, struggles for power, shifting alliances, and personal betrayals.

Overthrowing the Seleucid Kingdom was as formative for the Jewish worldview as the exodus from Egypt had been for earlier Israelites—a small group of people faced impossible odds to overthrow a large, domineering power. Increasingly, though, as the Hasmonean

Dynasty embraced Hellenism, people questioned if that was what God intended for a restored Jewish kingdom.

Then Rome arrived and established a new governing structure. The Jews were once more under the rule of a foreign empire, so what was meant by the biblical promises regarding the vindication of God's people? The Jews thought they were on the right path with kicking the Seleucids out of their land, but now a non-Jew ruled on behalf of Rome. What about the expected Jewish king from the line of David? Once again, people wondered what the concepts of repentance, return, and restoration looked like for the Jewish people. Speculations about another king or a "real" kingdom of God came with the hope that it would replace these suspect dynasties. People still hoped for a messiah who would rebuild the Davidic kingdom and usher the people into a new era.

For decades, the Jewish people discussed what real power looked like. Do you defeat the world by being better at the power game than everyone else? When Jesus began to teach about the kingdom of God, his statements were revolutionary. Jesus spoke about true power being a humble kind of inconvenient love, but that view was contrary to life as people experienced it. Embracing Jesus' vision was almost impossible for those who had recent memories of Greek, Hasmonean, and Roman governance.

4

Geography and Politics

In chapter 2, I discussed how the land was not an empty stage on which the human drama played out. The land of the Gospel narratives was an ecologically diverse place that, in effect, was another character in the biblical narrative, albeit one normally ignored. In chapter 3, I introduced the hidden agendas and political activities of the ruling parties that ended up shifting Jewish ideology. When these two topics—geography and politics—are considered together, they create a complex web of interlocking ideas that influenced how people heard Jesus' message about the kingdom of God.

As you read in the previous chapter, international policies were determined by the rise and fall of empires. The people in Judea were caught in the middle and were insignificant in the larger fight. After the death of Alexander the Great, this land became sandwiched between the Ptolemaic and the Seleucid kingdoms. The fall of the Seleucids came not from the small, Hasmonean resistance in Judea but from the international pressures from the growing Roman and Parthian Empires.

As a quick review, the land in the Gospels was a long, narrow strip compressed by the desert to the east and the sea to the west. It contained pockets of differing ecosystems that more easily separated people than brought them together. Significantly, the land did not produce a surplus of commodities, making it an unlikely incubator for a world-dominating empire. Instead, the land's importance emerged from the significant trade routes crossing within it. This was the terrain that *connected* superpowers, not *developed* them.

In addition to the land not uniting peoples, there was diversity in the population due to political actions. When the Jews returned to the hills of Judea, they were surrounded by a large variety of people groups who lived in these different ecosystems. To the north were the Samaritans, who descended from the people Assyria had transplanted to the region. To the south were the Idumeans, who descended from the Edomites and who moved into Judean territory once Babylon destroyed the Southern Kingdom. To the east were recently built Greco-Roman cities promoting a Hellenistic way of life.

The Hasmonean rulers tried to use forced conversion to hold the variety of people together under a cohesive government. While multiple people groups—such as the Idumeans, Samaritans, Judeans, Galileans, and Hellenists—lived in close proximity, they were not united by a singular sense of identity. Even among the Jews, there was a multitude of opinions about Torah interpretation or if the temple had been profaned by the Hasmonean leaders. With such divergent religious and cultural ideas in one land, developing a political structure capable of unifying everyone was almost impossible.

The Rise of Herod the Great

Figure 16. Imagined Depiction of Herod the Great (public domain).

One generation after Rome established dominance in the land, Herod, son of Antipas, entered the political arena. From the young age of twenty-five,

Herod demonstrated leadership by suppressing revolts and collecting taxes for Rome. He forcibly brought order to the Galilean provinces, captured Jerusalem, and beheaded Antigonus (the last Hasmonean who joined with the Parthians in revolt). While anyone who opposed Herod's rule was killed and their family wealth added to the royal coffers, anyone who supported his rule was richly rewarded. The Gospel writers refer to such supporters as the Herodians.

Herod became king around the same time Marc Antony controlled the Roman Empire and Cleopatra governed Egypt. Cleopatra tried to convince Antony to eliminate Herod and give her all of Herod's land. Although Antony did not dispose of Herod, he did give Cleopatra the wealth-producing lands around Jericho, the riches around the Dead Sea, and the enviable trade routes to Arabia. Animosity stirred in Herod's heart against Cleopatra, because she possessed the valuable parts of the territory that he insisted should belong to him. When Octavian defeated Antony, Herod saw an opportunity to regain this valuable terrain. Herod convinced the new Roman emperor to give him what used to belong to Cleopatra along with several additional Greco-Roman cities.

Herod was obsessively egotistical. Rome did not allow him to conquer new territory, and yet he wanted to prove his political prowess, so he built the seemingly impossible. Even now, two thousand years later, Herod is most notably remembered by the structures that challenged the very forces of nature—a three-tiered palace draped on the sheer cliff face of Masada, the Herodian fortress built on a high hill where such a hill did not previously exist, and the palace in Caesarea built on a submerged rock ledge protruding into the Mediterranean Sea. His architects brought revolutionary designs to the area—dome ceilings, circular structures, and harbor walls built from cement that solidified under water. He also built a site in Hebron to commemorate Israelite ancestors. Significantly, Herod expanded the platform on which the temple in Jerusalem was constructed. The sacred complex in Jerusalem became known throughout the Roman world for its uniqueness as the largest platform on which only one temple was built and in which no statue was placed.

As an Idumean, one of the people groups forced to convert to Judaism during the Hasmonean expansionist campaign, Herod was considered a half-Jew. But he tried to convince the Jewish people that he was the

long-awaited Messiah. He built a lavish building in Hebron to commemorate the Jewish patriarchs and their wives (except Rachel, who was buried
outside Bethlehem). He refurbished the Jerusalem temple to bring it to the
impressive glory the Jewish people believed it should have. He brought
the residents of his land into an era of relative prosperity. Although not in
the royal bloodline of David, Herod sat on the throne and built himself an
opulent palace in Jerusalem.

Consider the reoccurring pattern throughout history regarding the
construction of the temple[1] and the many great leaders who invested in it.
Solomon built the first temple, Joshua and Zerubbabel led the process of
building the Second Temple, and the Hasmoneans reclaimed it from foreign
rule, expanding it and making it more beautiful. Herod placed himself in
this line of rulers and tried to spin a messianic story around himself. No
one was fooled, though, because it was clear that Herod's true desire was
anything Rome offered. He gave the Jews their desired temple in Jerusalem,
but he also financed the building of opulent temples to Roman gods.

While Herod's actions were politically savvy, they were not appreciated
by all of his subjects. Animosity toward the half-Jewish ruler grew with each
passing year. Herod began his political career eliminating the Jewish rebellion against Rome and spent the rest of his career suspicious that friends,
family, and enemies alike were seeking opportunities take his kingdom away.

The Political Division of Herod the Great's Kingdom

Herod the Great was one of the few leaders able to semi-peacefully maintain
Roman control over such a diverse population, but he died before establishing which of his sons would inherit the kingdom. Six different times, Herod
designated an heir and wrote a will, but then a conspiracy theory circulated
that made Herod suspicious of a hostile takeover. Herod killed any person
he suspected of treason, including members of his own family. At the time
of his death, there was no valid will, so Rome divided Herod's territory into
four units that were governed by different leaders. This created the complex
political reality that existed during much of Jesus' life.

The king was gone, and people had not forgotten what independence
felt like. Without an obvious heir to the throne, the Jews saw an opportunity to resist the Roman presence in the land. Animosity toward Herod

prompted a small group of Jews to pull down the Roman eagles from the temple gates, and Rome retaliated by brutally slaying them.

When people from all over the empire came to Jerusalem to celebrate the Passover, they pressured Herod's son, Archelaus (we will discuss him in a moment), to take immediate action against the perpetrators of the brutal killings. Archelaus responded by sending soldiers to disperse the crowds. The ensuing conflict concluded with the soldiers massacring thousands of Jews. When Jewish pilgrims returned to Jerusalem on the next big Jewish holiday, Shavuot, people in the city and surrounding countryside staged a revolt against Rome. They too were stopped.

One man, who was Herod's servant, took advantage of the chaotic situation. Claiming to be the long-awaited Messiah, he gathered an army around himself and rebelled. Another obscure shepherd, of great physical prowess, also considered himself to be the Messiah and proceeded with his brothers to raid Roman and Herodian caravans. Each of these rebellions was squashed by Rome. Why mention these attempted insurrections? Primarily, because it is valuable for us to note that Jesus was not the first to claim to be the Messiah. There were others before him who all ended up as tragic, failed heroes. All the uprisings were stifled by Rome, and the more stifling Rome became, the more fervently people hoped for the Messiah.

Let us return to the political story at hand. Since Herod died without a will, Rome split up his territory into four parts. Herod's son, Archelaus, inherited Idumea, Judea, and Samaria—the primary core of the hill country. He was a ruthless ruler despised by all. When Joseph, Mary, and Jesus returned from Egypt, Joseph heard that Archelaus was in charge and took his family to Nazareth instead of staying in Bethlehem (see Matt. 2:22). The Judeans and Samaritans hated him so much that they set aside their animosity toward each other and sent a joint convoy to Rome with their complaints. Rome eventually exiled Archelaus to Gaul (modern France).

Subsequently, Roman governors were granted control of Archelaus's former territories of Idumea, Judea, and Samaria. They served a few years at a time before moving to another post. None of the governors liked living in the Jewish city of Jerusalem, so they moved their headquarters out to the Hellenized city of Caesarea on the Mediterranean coast. Both regions of Samaria and Judea retained conservative religious groups, each one holding tightly to their identity while also trying to benefit from their connection to Rome.

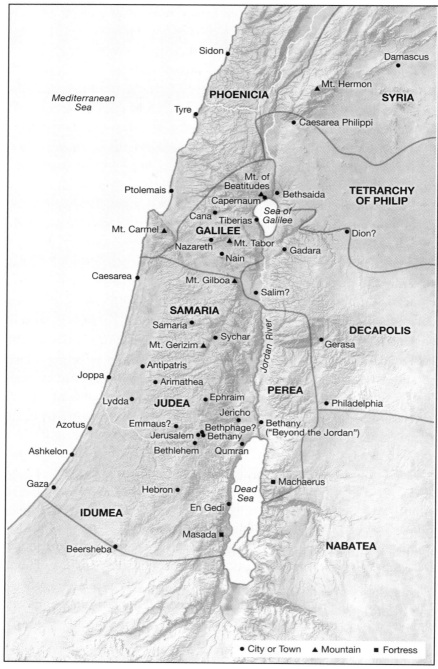

Figure 17. Herod's Kingdom Divided.

Herod's son, Herod Antipas (the Herod most often referenced in the Gospels), inherited the territories of Galilee, west of the Sea of Galilee, and Perea, east of the Jordan River. Although these two territories may seem to have nothing in common, their towns and villages similarly preserved a strong Jewish identity and culture. But, like his father, Antipas was influenced by Rome and subsidized the building of many Hellenized cities. So, although his political territories maintained a strong sense of Jewish identity, there were pockets of Roman imperial influence throughout.

Touching the northeastern edge of the Sea of Galilee and fanning out to the northeast was the territory of Gaulanitis. Herod's other son, Herod Philip, inherited Gaulanitis along with Iturea, Batanea, and Trachnitis. He expertly negotiated ruling a mixed population that included Roman citizens, Jewish zealots, and everyone in between.

Like Archelaus's territory, the fourth territory was given to Roman governors to rule instead of one of Herod's sons. The Decapolis ("ten cities"), as it was called, consisted of large cities without a strong Israelite narrative preserved in its landscape. These cities either embraced Hellenism when Alexander the Great passed through or were built with Hellenism as their foundation. Several of these cities were previously conquered during the Hasmonean expansionist campaign, but Pompey "released" them from Jewish control and turned them over to Roman governors. The Decapolis served as a physical and cultural barrier on Rome's eastern frontier.

Making Sense of Small Details

Jesus spent a lot of his time in Galilee, specifically around the Sea of Galilee, which is where three of the political units converged along the shores— Galilee, Gaulanitis, and the Decapolis. Galilee was primarily Jewish, the Decapolis was primarily Hellenistic, and Gaulanitis was a mixture of both. Each of the political units had different rulers. All of the residents, however, enjoyed the same freshwater resources, fish from the lake, and temperate climate. It is easy to imagine Jewish fishermen working through the night and then sorting fish in the early morning hours. Since their Jewish community would eat only kosher fish, what could they do with the nonkosher fish? Sell them to the Gentiles who did not have the same food preferences.

The people may have lived in different politically controlled areas, but that did not prevent them from interacting with one another.

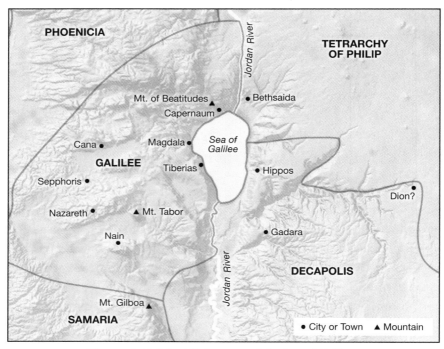

Figure 18. Political Units around the Sea of Galilee.

In the previous chapter on geography, we talked about Capernaum, the Jewish town that was built on the northern shoreline of the Sea of Galilee. Although it was in the political unit of Galilee, it was close to the border with Gaulanitis. While fishermen, farmers, and skilled craftsmen lived there because of the rich natural resources, Roman soldiers and tax collectors were there because of politics. Herod Antipas controlled Galilee, and Herod Philip controlled Gaulanitis, and they both collected taxes for Rome (and themselves). Capernaum was the last town in Galilee before crossing into Philip's territory, so there should be no surprise that when Jesus left "his own city" of Capernaum, he immediately found Matthew, a tax collector. What would have been a surprise, however, was that Jesus asked a tax collector to be his disciple (Matt. 9:9; Mark 2:14; Luke 5:27).

The small size of the lake surrounded by elevated hills gave interested observers a chance to follow Jesus' travels from one shoreline to another.

Until I saw the Sea of Galilee, I never understood how people could race ahead of Jesus and be on the shore when he arrived. My mental picture for a lake was based on huge, freshwater mountain lakes, which is nothing like the Sea of Galilee, where the entire shoreline is visible from the hillside. The Gospel writers use the phrase "crossing to the other side" to indicate when Jesus moved from one geopolitical unit to another, which does not always indicate a great distance.[2] When Jesus and the disciples traveled by boat and "crossed to the other side," the crowds of people were able to see where they were going and could easily ran ahead to meet Jesus where he landed.

Even today, you could sit on the shores of the Sea of Galilee, read the Gospel of Mark, and imagine the events playing out on the terrain around you. Jesus spent most of his time around those shores, and the geographical context around the Sea of Galilee allowed Jesus to reach a wide audience. He interacted with a variety of people with different assumptions, lifestyles, politics, and religion. With such diversity, the Sea of Galilee was like a microcosm of the Roman Empire. It was an ideal training ground for the disciples, who would later be tasked with spreading the good news throughout the world. After years of watching Jesus interact with people and absorbing his teachings, the disciples were well prepared for the task.

Comparing Galilee and Decapolis

Understanding the geopolitical fragmentation of the land during Jesus' life illuminates some of the hidden drama in the Gospels. As Jesus traveled between political units, he modified his interactions with people depending on the context. If we are not aware of this political geography, however, Jesus' interactions with people may seem inconsistent to us. For instance, while in Galilee, Jesus healed people and then asked them not to tell anyone what he had done. When Jesus healed people in the Decapolis, though, he told them to tell everyone. Using the political information above makes plain what initially may seem to be confusing. Context is the key!

The Jewish people in regions like Galilee anticipated a God-anointed, human agent who would restore the Jewish kingdom. For some Jews, that expectation included what previous messiahs were unable to do—overthrow Roman rule and reestablish a kingdom like King David's. Within this politically charged context, Jesus performed miracles as evidence of the arrival of

God's kingdom. Jesus embodied the role of Messiah, but he also taught that the role did not include a violent overthrow of Rome as the people expected. He restored people physically, socially, and spiritually, which supported the idea of God's kingdom, but he did not advocate for a revolt and did not want the crowds to make him king by force (John 6:15). This is why he told those people not to spread the word about his deeds.

In contrast, when Jesus was in the Decapolis, he interacted with those with a different worldview. Birthed from Hellenistic ideology, the Decapolis's residents were not waiting for a messiah nor were they hoping for a human agent to lead a revolt against Rome. While the people here recognized that Jesus' actions were extraordinary, this did not mean they wanted to enthrone him. They did not associate Jesus' actions with a political agenda. Therefore, Jesus encouraged people of the Decapolis to spread the news about him.

Reading the Gospels with an awareness of the different political regions also helps us uncover more of the gospel message. All Four Gospels describe the miraculous feeding of the five thousand with bread and fish (Matt. 14:13–21; Mark 6:32–44; Luke 9:10–17; John 6:1–15). This is the miracle discussed in chapter 2, where we focused on Passover as an important backdrop for Jesus' actions. Although the geographical details given in the Gospels is complex, the event likely happened along the edge of Galilee. The crowds were organized in groups of fifty and a hundred, just like the Israelites coming out of Egypt. Jesus provided food in a remote place, and twelve baskets of bread were left over, perhaps representing provision for the twelve Israelite tribes. The miracle is rich with the pattern of the Exodus event and invites us to ponder the important part Jesus played in the drama.

Matthew and Mark record a second miracle of feeding the crowds, but I like to think that this time the miracle took place in the Decapolis (Matt. 15:29–39; Mark 8:1–10). I mentioned above how different the mind-set of the Hellenized Decapolis was from Jewish Galilee. And when Jesus fed the four thousand, there were no Israelite undertones to the story. However, Jesus fed them just as he had fed his Jewish audience. Seven baskets of food were left over, and we should ask ourselves why that number. Seven is a perfect number, but also during this time the phrase "seven nations" was used to refer to all the Gentiles. The reference comes from Deuteronomy 7:1, which lists the "seven nations larger and stronger than you." If the twelve baskets of leftovers from the first miracle represented provision for the twelve tribes, then it is likely that the seven baskets of food in this miracle represented provision for all the rest of the nations. What Jesus did for the Jews, he also did for the Gentiles.

Comparing Galilee and Judea

As we have seen, Galilee was quite different from the Decapolis, but it was also different from Judea, even though the majority of people in these regions had a Jewish worldview. Do you recall the earlier discussion about how geography influences how open or closed a community may be to new ideas? Those who lived with open horizon lines and access to international influences—like people in Galilee—were more willing to accommodate the views of outsiders than those who lived with tight horizon lines and little international access. In addition, people in Galilee were land-oriented, subsistence-living people who felt the oppressive hand of Rome. This region was therefore an incubator for ideas of resistance. The geographical influence and the political views of people in Galilee meant crowds followed Jesus and congregated in open fields to listen to his message about God's kingdom.

In contrast, the hills of Judea—with their short horizon lines and difficult roads—were home to a conservative society that changed slowly. Jerusalem was urban, but it had the temple and the Israelite narrative firmly rooted in the ground. The political and wealthy elite lived here, who embraced elements of Hellenistic ideals that came with more power and influence over the masses. Therefore, the inhabitants of the Judean hills and the aristocratic elite in Jerusalem were skeptical of Jesus and reluctant to embrace his new ideas. Kingdom of God discussions in Jerusalem—the location of the temple and the Jewish religious center, but also where the elite who enjoyed Roman connections lived—led to heated debates about Jesus' teaching agenda.

One technical point needs to be made here. The Greek word Ἰουδαιοι can be translated as "Judean" or as "Jew"—after all, it was the Israelites from the geographical region of Judah who were taken into exile in Babylon who later were called Judeans or Jews. When modern translators interpret the Greek New Testament, they decide when to translate the Greek word

Ἰουδαιοι into the English word *Jew* or *Judean*, and that choice has a powerful effect on how the reader understands the narrative.

For example, John 7:1 says, "After this Jesus went about in Galilee. He would not go about in Judea, because the Ἰουδαιοι were seeking to kill him." If a translator chooses the word *Jew*, this then is a comprehensive statement that implies that all of the Jews were seeking to kill Jesus. But notice the geography mentioned in the text. Jesus went about in *Galilee*, but he would not go about in *Judea*. Based on the explanation of Galilee in this chapter, you know that they were primarily Jewish. Therefore, it does not make sense to say that Jesus walked about freely in Galilee but not Judea because the *Jews* were trying to kill him. "The Jews" lived in Galilee too! John 7:1 is making a *geographical* statement. Jesus found the crowds (of Jews) in Galilee more accepting of his message than the crowds (of Jews) in Judea.

Kingdom of God and Kingdom of Rome

There is another interesting narrative that fits in this geopolitical chapter. Matthew 16 says that Jesus took his disciples out of (Jewish) Galilee to go to the vicinity of Caesarea Philippi. It is important to know two facts about Caesarea Philippi: the city was located in Gaulanitis, and the city was built with Hellenism at its core. Herod Philip built the city according to Roman values and ideals. He dedicated it to Caesar and then added his own name at the end (hence Caesarea Philippi). At the core of the city was a huge, pagan worship complex dedicated to Caesar and to the god Pan.

There are many beautiful things about the narrative in Matthew 16, but let us focus on the political geography of the story. Jesus and his disciples stood in an area where everything about a dominant, human-styled kingdom was on display: worship of other gods, worship of leaders, opulent wealth, and self-aggrandizement. It was in this location that Jesus asked the disciples who people thought he was. They responded, "Some say John the Baptist; others say Elijah; and still others, Jeremiah or one of the prophets" (v. 14). Then Jesus asked those who had lived life with him and learned from his actions as well as his teachings, "But what about you? . . . Who do you say that I am?" Peter correctly identified Jesus as the Messiah, but he clearly misunderstood what that meant. Like so many others, the disciples thought the role of the Messiah was to be the liberator of the Jews from Rome's control. Can you feel the tension rising? I wonder if Peter was thinking that this Roman city was the perfect place to declare a revolt against Rome.

But then Jesus made a dramatic and unexpected revelation: he told his disciples that as the Messiah, he would return to Jerusalem and be put to death. None of those words would make sense in a first-century Jewish context. Only failed messiahs were killed by Rome. How could God restore his people and bring about his kingdom on earth if God's chosen leader died? Peter was the bold one to voice what others probably thought: "This shall never happen to you!" (Matt. 16:22).

Jesus, however, was not declaring a revolt against Rome; he was explaining how God's kingdom would finally conquer evil. By making this statement in Caesarea Philippi, Jesus compared a Roman-styled empire to the kingdom of God. Rome put everything about human ingenuity, power, and wealth on display. But God's kingdom would be ushered in by the one willing to embark on a journey of inconvenient and generous love. Rome's empire was built on the backs of slaves. God's kingdom was built through sacrifice and justice.

Without understanding the object lesson, Peter protested that Jesus' view must not be right. Jesus replied with the rebuke, "Get behind me, Satan!" (v. 23). That sounds quite harsh to say to a disciple who not only previously voiced the truth of Jesus' messiahship but who was also one of Jesus' trusted friends and a star pupil. Maybe Jesus recognized in Peter's words a similar temptation to what he had faced in the Judean wilderness at the beginning of his ministry. At that time, Satan tempted Jesus to be the type of messiah who prioritized self-advancement and self-preservation, but Jesus refused (we will discuss this further in chapter 7). Three years later, at the end of his public ministry, Jesus still rejected that version of the messianic role.

Conclusion

Jesus lived in a complex society. The small land through which he walked with his disciples was filled with a variety of ecosystems, political units, and worldviews. In chapter 8, we will discuss how brilliant Jesus was to be able to communicate to such diverse groups of people. But in this chapter, we laid the foundation for the significance of not only asking *what* happened in the narrative but also *where* it happened.

5

LIFELONG LEARNING

In this chapter, we will combine several lessons from earlier chapters to think specifically about Jewish life at the time of Jesus. The exile had a tremendous impact on Jewish identity, and so too did the waves of Hellenism that crashed onto the eastern shores of the Mediterranean Sea. Judaism became the minority cultural identity embedded in the more powerful majority culture of Hellenism. Since the Jews no longer had kingdom borders to define them, they turned to social behaviors to separate them from the communities around them.

We would be more accurate if we started speaking of Judaisms (plural) due to the diversity of beliefs. As is evident from the geography chapters, some of the diversity was place driven. Those who lived in the hills, near the temple, close to massive Roman cities, or dispersed throughout the Roman Empire all developed their own ideas of what it meant to embody the role of God's people in the world. Jews came to different conclusions about what defined purity or what it meant to live faithfully according to the covenant. They agreed that individuals were responsible for Torah obedience, but they disagreed on the connection between individual behavior and rituals at the temple. This chapter explains the overall shape of society—but reader, beware. Even here, I paint with large brushstrokes. The reality of lived life would have been more nuanced than I can cover here. However, this generalized backdrop will be valuable for part 2 of the book when we seek to understand Jesus' life as a dynamic Jewish teacher.

Jewish Life

The wealthy minority lived in large homes in an urban context. Their dwellings were extensive, with inner courtyards, and they imbued a sense of

luxury characterized by expensive artistic works such as ornamental fres-
coes, stucco work, mosaic floors, and bathing facilities. The craftsmanship
of the homes, along with the expensive household goods used inside the
homes, reflect an affinity the elite had for a lifestyle similar to the Romans
in Pompeii.[1] These families had a high standard of living. It is interesting to
note that many of Jesus' opponents were from this wealthy elite, who had a
lot to lose if he gained too much popular support.

Life for most people in Jesus' community was difficult. As was common
in agrarian societies, the small social elite ruled over the much larger lower
class, who produced food and goods for them. The lower class primarily consisted of outdoor people—fishermen, traders, farmers, and crafters.
They lived close to nature. Most people relied on subsistence living from
the land and struggled for survival.[2]

Social norms were distinguished mostly by status and not necessarily by
gender, as many modern people assume when they talk about Jesus interacting with women. Therefore, taking a moment to address the role of women
in society is worthwhile, because the widely circulated comments of women
being completely oppressed and invisible in a patriarchal, Jewish society
are not entirely accurate. In recent years, scholars such as Carol Meyers and
Lynn Cohick have done tremendous research that enables us to nuance some
of the broad, sweeping statements about women's participation in society.[3]

While it is true that society was patriarchal and that women were defined in relation to their male relatives, this does not mean that women were
forced into seclusion. After all, the majority of people relied on subsistence
living. Everyone needed to contribute to the survival of the household and
extended family. Women were not hidden in the house but instead had significant public engagements, and they sometimes worked alongside their
husbands in the family business.[4] They worked in public shops, were em-
ployed as wet nurses, and became patrons of the trades.

Women were fully integrated into synagogue congregations and participated with men in synagogue life.[5] A separate gendered space did not exist
in the early synagogues, and thus there was no divider or "women's balcony."
We do have evidence of early synagogues that had balconies, but there is
no proof that it was for the women instead of being a section for latecom-
ers or overflow. Women participated in study sessions in the *bet midrash*
(house of learning) and were not prevented from attaining great learning.

Jesus accepted women, taught them, and honored them, but it is important to realize that his actions were not in contrast to how they were treated in those days.[6] When we see women supporting Jesus' ministry, following him like a disciple, and sitting at his feet to learn, we see a reflection of the norm in Jewish society and not a way in which Jesus contradicted his culture.

Learning as Worship

In the wider Hellenistic society, education was primarily the prerogative of the wealthy class. If a student needed a particular knowledge or skill, the tutor arranged for intellectual studies. If the body needed training, then physical exercises were arranged in the gymnasium.[7] In contrast, Jewish education was viewed as benefiting the whole person's being and thus significant for every person in the community. "The Greeks learned in order to comprehend. The Hebrews learned in order to revere."[8] The goal of education in Jewish communities was not to acquire intellectual abilities as much as to value submission to authority of Scripture and to learn radical obedience to God, which was viewed as the best form of wisdom.

The value of education was therefore deeply imbedded in Jewish thought. Instructing children in God's law was an integral part of the Torah. Deuteronomy 6 and 11 instruct parents to teach God's commands "when you sit at home and when you walk along the road, when you lie down and when you get up" (Deut. 6:7; 11:19). In other words, all of the time! Understandably, the trauma of exile served to underscore the importance of such learning in the home. Education was viewed as the strength of the nation and essential for survival.

In chapter 1, I mentioned that synagogues developed during the time of the Babylonian exile. The Israelites were scattered throughout the Babylonian territories, and without the temple to crystalize their Jewish identity, they shifted their focus to the biblical text. They studied at home but also added times to study together. During a synagogue service, someone read the Torah out loud to the gathered community. If necessary, the Hebrew text was translated into Aramaic. An elder or scholar then led a discussion about the Scripture in which everyone participated. People were not told to blindly accept and follow the teaching. They were prompted to meditate on it and to derive the deeper meaning of the text.

Synagogue buildings became a house of study for the whole community (men, women, and children). You may remember from the previous chapter that when Salome Alexandra was the Hasmonean queen of Judea, she commanded that all children should attend school. As Josephus writes:

> Our principle care of all is this, to educate our children well; and we think it to be the most necessary business of our whole life to observe the laws that have been given us, and to keep those rules of piety that have been delivered down to us.[9]

Each Jewish community had an educational space that was near the synagogue or attached to the synagogue as a side room. The clearest evidence suggests that Jewish communities created three levels of education for children. The first level was called the *bet sepher* (house of the scroll) where all children as young as five learned the Torah. They started with memorizing the *Shema*, the Creation narratives of Genesis 1–5, and the essence of Levitical law (Lev. 1–8). Perhaps teaching small children Levitical law sounds strange, but the rabbis considered young children to be pure. In Leviticus, sacrifices are pure and therefore, the rabbis said, the pure should study the pure (Leviticus Rabbah 7:3).

Rabbinic tradition informs us that educators used honey in a special ceremony on the first day of school. Young children were shown a slate, and on it was the alphabet and the statement "The Law will be my calling" (Lev 1:1 and Deut. 33:4). The teacher read the words, and the child repeated them. Then the slate was covered in honey, and the child licked the honey from the slate. By doing so, the child learned early on that the word of God was as sweet as honey in the mouth (Prov. 24:13-14a; Ps. 119:103; Ezek. 3:3).[10]

Not every child attended the second level of learning, however, which was called the *bet talmud* (house of learning). By the age of ten, young girls spent all their time with their mothers learning how to manage a household, and some boys began to learn the family trade from their fathers. Only the boys with an aptitude for study remained in school to learn the art of asking good, probing questions. They finished memorizing Scripture and began to engage the Oral Law. Jesus was about this age when his parents took him to Jerusalem to celebrate Passover. At the conclusion of the celebration, Mary and Joseph left the city in a caravan of friends and family without realizing

Jesus was not with them. When they realized their mistake, they returned to the city and found him in the temple, listening to the elders *and asking them good questions* (Luke 2:46).

Think of all the times Jesus began interactions with people by asking a question. Such engagements were knit into the Jewish culture. Questions invite people into a conversation of inquiry instead of rote memorization. Questioning the meaning in the text and questioning each other's conclusions was not rude but showed curiosity and interest. Students were allowed to argue with their teachers, as long as it was done with a reverent attitude and not with a contentious spirit.

The third level of education was reserved for the brightest of the boys. Students age thirteen and above attended the *bet midrash* (house of study). In their spare time, they studied with the teachers of the law in the process of mastering the law. They learned about the relationship between the written Torah and the Oral Law, and they were taught how to investigate the meaning of Scripture and debate with their teachers.

Learning did not end when the student left the educational program. The Jewish community promoted a lifelong education, with the Torah as the only textbook needed. The Mishnah is a compilation of Jewish text dating after Jesus' time, but the writings reflect the attitude that permeated earlier Jewish culture. "If thou wantest advice—even in matters secular or in questions regarding behavior and good manners—take it from the Torah" (Pesiq. Rab Kah. 105a). "Turn it [the Torah] and turn it over again, for everything is in it, and contemplate it, and wax gray and old over it, and stir not from it, for thou canst have no better rule than this" (Avot 5:25).

People gathered in homes or in the synagogue to engage traveling teachers in conversation over the meaning of the Torah. "Let your house be a meeting-place for the sages, and sit in the very dust at their feet, and thirstily drink in their words" (Avot 1:4). The story of Jesus staying in Mary and Martha's house, and prioritizing the learning of Scripture, depicts a common scene in Jewish life (Luke 10:38–42; see also Acts 22:3). Every person's calling was to education and, significantly, learning happened in community and not on one's own.

The Jewish view of the Scriptures was different from our modern-day Greek philosophy-inspired perspective. Many Western Christians try to "solve" the text by establishing linear ways of logic to come to a final conclusion of what the text means. Jews, on the other hand, from the early childhood days of education were taught the value of exploring the text with questions and then discussing the questions with others in the community. They sought to pull open and explore the infinite depth of the text, not "solve" the meaning of the text.

Following a Master-Teacher

Few students had an incredible mental acuity for engaging Scripture and the oral traditions. Those students had a life-changing opportunity to learn from a master-teacher, only if the student found a teacher willing to take the student under his wing. Shmuel Safrai notes that study by itself did not transform a student into a disciple. There were subjects which could not be systematically studied or explicitly enunciated. The student learned the nuances of his master's spiritual teachings only by participating in the master's life.[11] A true disciple left everything—their families, wives, homes, careers, and communities—to live, travel, and minister with their teacher. The goal was to participate in and share life with him, and in doing so learn to ingest subtle spiritual matters. The relationship between rabbi and student was of utmost importance, even greater than that with family. "The father had given the physical features. The master would sculpt the soul."[12] The father shaped the boy for this world, but the teacher shaped the student for eternity.

The teacher scheduled times with students to review and learn, but living life with the teacher also provided spontaneous times of teaching. Time spent walking between villages was probably filled with impromptu conversations and mulling over ideas, and the physical land became visual aids and object lessons (this will be explored more in chapter 8). Learning from an expert teacher was certainly not an education defined by rooms, exams, and degrees, but by life. Disciples not only absorbed the wisdom of the teacher, but they also learned to *live* like the teacher. It was experiential education at its best.

Sometimes when I have a tour group in Israel and we are about to embark on a hike, I ask them to be mindful of what happens among our group before we arrive at the destination point. At the end of the hike, the group reflects on their time. Some individuals try to find solitude to contemplate the day, while others engage in stimulating conversations with fellow hikers.

People walking near me often ask follow-up questions from lessons earlier in the day. This practice of paying attention to the *in-between* moments is helpful for imagining what life was like for a disciple and his teacher. The simple moments in the day provided perfect teaching opportunities.

Jesus taught in synagogues, temple courts, private houses, and in the open countryside. He taught his disciples by embodying his theology, asking provoking questions, and then clarifying his ideas. Jesus taught in words and in action, as is evident even among the crowds who comment on Jesus' "new teaching"—not after *hearing* his spoken words but after *seeing* his deeds.[13] A great number of people highly respected Jesus as a teacher, which prompted many to refer to him with the honorable title "Rabbi" in the same manner as they would use "Teacher" or "Master."

A Difference of Opinion

In chapter 3, I hinted at the growing fragmentation in Judaism that came about as reactions to developments in their current events. Now is a good time to look more intentionally at these sects within Judaism.[14] And yet here, too, I am in danger of oversimplifying for the sake of brevity.

The Sadducee sect grew out of the wealthy, priestly class that viewed themselves as the descendants of Zadok the priest (2 Sam. 8:17; 15:24; 1 Kings 4:4). Sadducees controlled temple life and were personally invested in the political world and the continued influence of the Roman Empire in Jerusalem. As such, they were immensely offended when Jesus spoke out against the temple (Mark 11:15–19; 14:57–58; 15:29). The Sadducees were well educated, politically savvy, and the early adopters of Hellenism. In many ways, they complied with the cultural forces of the day to advance their own power and influence. When interpreting Scripture, the Sadducees held sacred the Torah of Moses but rejected the writings of the prophets or the oral traditions. They trusted the ancient Israelite law code but considered everything else to be interpretation and therefore not authoritative.

Remember the story of Jason from chapter 3? He was the first to pay for the role of high priest during Seleucid rule. At that time, the Essenes formed due to a strong reaction against the perceived corruption of the political and religious leaders. The Essenes wanted to honor God, temple, and Torah, but they believed that the evolution of the high priesthood and the Sadducees' connection to politics corrupted the temple. They abhorred the increasing influence of Hellenism in the Jewish culture. The prophets promised that a remnant would survive and that through the remnant, God would bring about restoration. When the Essenes read Scripture, they understood Isaiah 40–55 as a clue to how God would redeem the true remnant of Israel: through repentance, trust, and obedience. They believed they were that remnant because they alone maintained a pure and obedient lifestyle. They read the exclamation in Isaiah 40:3, to prepare a way in the wilderness for the return of God to his city, as pertaining to them. So, they withdrew and waited for the Messiah. They lived as separatists and developed their own communities, in which they maintained a strict code of purity, piety, and study.

Do you remember the Hasidim? They were the faithful ones determined to take God's laws seriously to prepare for restoration and to prevent another catastrophe like the exile. They refused to fight the Seleucids on the Sabbath until Mattathias convinced them otherwise. Once the temple in Jerusalem was restored (under Judas Maccabaeus), the Hasidim returned to a religious life, not a military or political one. The Pharisees evolved from this group. Pharisees were not from the priestly line, but they cared deeply about the Torah and sought to interpret God's instructions with care.

The Jewish historian Josephus described the Pharisees as an influential and popular group that had a reputation of excellence and high ideals. His positive view of them may be due in part to the fact that he identified himself as a Pharisee. They were well respected by the people, and they esteemed the teachings of their elders. The Pharisees taught that it was imperative for Jewish people to understand their heritage, to preserve social distinctions, and to separate themselves from sin.[15] The Pharisees also had enormous respect for the sacred text and for the process of interpreting it for their modern culture. They accepted the tradition of interpretation all the way from ancient times to the oral traditions of their day. While the Sadducees had the power and wealth associated with the temple, the Pharisees had broad-based support among the people. While the Essenes isolated themselves from the majority of society, the Pharisees prioritized holiness within the community.

While Jesus never identified himself as a Pharisee, his conversations about angels and demons, the inspiration of all of Scripture, and the resurrection of the dead have the most in common with this sect of Judaism.

The Gospels record many disputes between the Pharisees and Jesus over an external display of piety through tithing, fasting, purity, and Sabbath observance. Jesus, however, was not completely at odds with the Pharisees. He commended their conclusions on Scriptures, but he also pointed to the gap between what they concluded about Scripture and how they lived their lives (Matt. 23). Jesus valued holiness in daily life, but he emphasized the heart attitude as reflected in action over rote adherence to laws.[16] Jesus demonstrated a zeal for the Torah but opposed the type of nationalism the Pharisees promoted.[17] Jesus' conflict with the religious hypocrisy of his day placed him *deeper* within the observant Jewish context not in contrast to it.

A portion of the Pharisees followed in the footsteps of their Hasmonean ancestors and embraced a militaristic, violent approach to establishing God's kingdom. They were known as the Zealots. According to Josephus, an uprising initiated by Judas Gaulanite and Saddok the Pharisee "sowed the seed" of trouble and began the Zealot movement, which Josephus considered to be "an intrusive school of philosophy."[18] The Zealots rejected Roman taxation, and they took on the slogan "No king but God!" They were not going to wait for God's deliverance and considered it their duty to pick up their swords and fight.

Points of Debate

The Torah gives instructions such as not working on the Sabbath (Exod. 20:8–10), but what exactly was "work" and who decided this? At what point did a pleasurable walk down a road to visit neighbors become work? After one kilometer or five? Cooked food was necessary for the family on the Sabbath, but women were included in the instructions not to work. At what point, then, was preparing food work? Harvesting crops was certainly work, but what if a person was hungry and they hand-picked a little grain when they walked through a field? Jesus was brought into such debates with the Pharisees. Readers of the Gospels would do well to resist the urge to view these encounters as if Jesus was a holy man of God and the Pharisees were evil men. These debates were between God-fearing Jewish leaders who sought to interpret Scriptures correctly.

The Torah commands parents to circumcise all newborn males eight days after birth (Gen. 17:12). But what if the eighth day fell on a Sabbath when all work was forbidden? Which command should the parents break? Or, rather, which command had precedence? The religious leaders determined that one should keep the command to circumcise on the eighth day, even if the day landed on a Sabbath. Jesus used such conclusions in John 7:23 to justify his decision to heal on the Sabbath: "Now if a boy can be circumcised on the Sabbath so that the law of Moses may not be broken, why are you angry with me for healing a man's whole body on the Sabbath?"

Again, a question regarding the Sabbath arose when interpreting the instruction in Deuteronomy 22:4, which states that a person should rescue an animal from a pit even if the animal is not theirs. But what if the animal was found on the Sabbath? Should the person adhere to the Sabbath rest or rescue the animal? Jesus claimed, as other rabbis did, that preserving life superseded the Sabbath commands. Jesus used that reasoning to address his own actions on the Sabbath. Jesus healed a man with a shriveled hand; and in response to questions by the religious leaders who were probing into his view of the Sabbath, Jesus replied, "If any of you has a sheep and it falls into a pit on the Sabbath, will you not take hold of it and lift it out? How much more valuable is a person than a sheep! Therefore it is lawful to do good on the Sabbath" (Matt. 12:11–12).

Arguments also surrounded the proper interpretation of purity laws. Since each of the popular sects of Judaism required different degrees of adherence to the law, you can imagine the possible conflicts between what people identified as morally clean or unclean. Jesus ate and drank with all kinds of people and in many different sorts of contexts—from celebrations in homes to meals in open fields. Jesus ate with prominent leaders and also those who were not considered respectable society. Think about how that could easily stir up debate with the Pharisees, who adamantly supported holiness within the community. When Jesus came in contact with those who were unclean, many pious leaders thought Jesus was disrespecting the accepted interpretation of Scripture. And remember, since the Babylonian exile when God's people no longer had a kingdom with boundaries, social behavior had become a valued part of distinguishing themselves from other people. Some people observed Jesus' actions as blurring the lines between those who demonstrated their love for God through faithful adherence to purity laws and those who did not.

Debates went beyond the proper interpretation of the law. For instance, people disagreed on what God's restoration would be like. The prophets and interpreters of the law repeated that the people must *repent, return,* and then God would *restore* them, but how did the people know if they had properly repented or returned to God? Where was the restoration? In their long history, when Egypt or foreign nations oppressed the Israelites, God delivered his people through mighty acts and brought them through trials to their vindication. In Jesus' day, there were mixed attitudes about the rulers, politics, and religion. The Essenes separated themselves from society, Sadducees were Hellenistic and Jewish, and the Zealots wanted action and decided to actively fight foreign rule by picking up swords and not paying taxes.

Jesus offered a different view. His teachings and his actions affirmed the idea that God was fixing all of creation through his chosen people. Unlike the Essenes or the Zealots, however, Jesus did not teach that the political enemy would be conquered. Jesus focused on the fact that in God's kingdom, God's people would finally fulfill their intended identity as the people of God for the world.

Conclusion

What can be said about the overall shape of life in Jesus' community? It was difficult. People were intimately connected to the land. Broadly speaking, the Jews prioritize learning Torah even though there were diverse opinions about what was considered sacred text and how to interpret it. Jesus fit within this diversity. The Gospels portray him interacting with the wealthy elite and with the common poor. People were curious about Jesus' interpretation of Scripture. Jesus had disciples who memorized and ingested his way of life, and at the end of Jesus' life, he told his disciples to go and become leaders and teachers of others.

Part Two

Reading Jesus in Context

6

BIRTH NARRATIVE

When I ask people to summarize the narrative of Jesus' birth, they start with Mary and Joseph traveling alone to Bethlehem. Mary is nine months pregnant, and yet somehow she is comfortably riding on a donkey. Unnecessarily cruel innkeepers in Bethlehem slam doors in the face of the young couple, until one man begrudgingly shows compassion and allows them to crash in the barn behind the house. They are alone when Mary gives birth. Baby Jesus sleeps peacefully in a wooden, straw-filled manger inside an A-frame barn with a donkey, some sheep, and a cow in attendance. Finally, shepherds arrive along with three gift-laden wise men to gaze at the baby. The scene is peaceful, reverent, and holy. Does this sound familiar?

Would you be surprised to know that very few of those details are actually present in the narrative? I'm serious! Go back to Luke 2:1–16 and read carefully. Look for the donkey. Look for the innkeeper. Pay attention to how far along Mary is in her pregnancy. Most of the details we associate with Jesus' birth do not come from the biblical text but from our culture. We absorb ideas about the nativity scene through seasonal Christmas cards, carols, and church reenactments. The images are so ingrained that we do not notice the discrepancies between our mental picture and the biblical narrative. Additionally, when we read the text, we do not always understand the implied cultural details from that time. In Luke 2, there is no donkey nor an innkeeper. Mary was probably not nine months pregnant when she walked to Bethlehem, and the birth scene was most likely busy and filled with people. A more realistic picture of the nativity, therefore, requires a fresh look at the biblical narrative within the political, cultural, and geographical context we have learned thus far.

Of the Four Gospels, only Matthew and Luke describe Jesus' birth. Each focuses on different details.[1] When read together, they enhance our understanding of when and where Jesus was born, and they foreshadow Jesus' role in God's narrative.

Geography and Narrative

Both Matthew and Luke specify that Bethlehem was the birthplace of Jesus. Bethlehem was located five miles south of Jerusalem along the spine of the hill country. From this location, inhabitants watched clouds form over the Mediterranean Sea and release precipitation as the air currents cooled when they flowed over the mountains. The rain tapered off east of Bethlehem, where the ground dropped away into the Rift Valley. Although it received an amount of rain adequate for agriculture, the village was vulnerable to the desiccating effects of the wilderness to the east and drought was a common threat. This insecurity prompted residents to diversify their assets to benefit from both farming and shepherding industries.[2] This tough land supported sheep and goats but not larger animals.

Bethlehem was on the primary local route, but its unpredictable agricultural ability and its lack of significant east or west connections meant that it was historically overshadowed by the larger cities of Jerusalem to the north and Hebron to the south. This small village was the hometown of the King David, the shepherd boy who achieved greatness as Israel's king. Otherwise, Bethlehem was not noteworthy geographically, agriculturally, or commercially—a concept the Old Testament prophets recognized. The prophet Micah wrote, "But you, Bethlehem Ephrathah, . . . are small among the clans of Judah" (Mic. 5:2a). The statement is an accurate comment on the unimpressive nature of the village. Nevertheless, Micah goes on to remark that the town had significant promise. Why? "Out of you will come for me one who will be ruler over Israel, whose origins are from of old, from ancient times" (Mic. 5:2b). The future Messiah, the one from the lineage of King David, would come from Bethlehem. Micah expressed hope that the future leader, born in the small village, would bring restoration to God's people.

Matthew and Luke knew of such writings from the prophets. Both authors therefore specify that Bethlehem was the location for Jesus' birth and thus created the first layer in the argument that Jesus was the expected messiah. Now, of course, not every person born in Bethlehem was immediately connected to David, so Matthew and Luke had to fashion another layer in their story to demonstrate that Jesus was born into David's royal lineage.[3]

Genealogies and Narrative

Matthew and Luke each provide Jesus' genealogy, albeit in their own unique style. The writers choose different people to include as a way of highlighting significant aspects of Jesus' family. Now, I realize that genealogical lists in the Bible seem drab and unnecessarily tedious. However, genealogies are like little packets of information strung together to create a story, with each name representing a moment in Israel's history. When read together, the list of names creates a personal narrative of the family's experiences with God. The two genealogies for Jesus in the Gospels not only demonstrate that Jesus' life was connected to the larger Israelite storyline, but they also foreshadow the greatness to come in the life of Jesus.

Matthew begins with a provocative, introductory statement: Jesus is the Messiah who is the son of David who is the son of Abraham. Mentioning David and Abraham together creates a link between the long-cherished images of an ideal king (David) with images of the respected Israelite patriarch (Abraham). Matthew follows the statement with a stylized genealogy to support his point—but "stylized" does not mean false. Matthew persuasively tells his narrative with carefully edited information in the genealogy.

The list begins with Abraham and progresses to Jesus. Matthew lists fourteen generations from Abraham to David, another fourteen generations from David to the exile, and fourteen more from the exile to Jesus. This threefold division organizes the genealogy around the high and low points of Israel's history—Abraham, David, and the trauma of exile. The repetitive use of the number "fourteen" further underscores Jesus' connection to David, because fourteen is the number associated with David's name. In ancient times, letters were assigned numerical values. The first letter of the Hebrew alphabet was 1, the second letter 2, and so on. Also, words in Hebrew were written only with consonants. David's name in Hebrew is דוד. If we apply the numbers to the consonants, then ד is four and ו is six. The numbers for David's name (ד ו ד) are $4 + 6 + 4 = 14$. So, the entire genealogical list supports the statement Matthew makes in the first verse. Jesus belonged to (and was the culmination of) the Israelite story that began with

Abraham and continued through King David through whom the Messiah would come.

Matthew's craftsmanship goes even deeper. A surprising collection of people are included in the list—sinful kings, righteous kings, marginalized people, and women. Matthew rejected the traditional method of documenting lineage only through the firstborn sons. We should ask what advantage is gained by Matthew going off-script. Take the women's names, for instance. Including women in a genealogy is shocking enough, but more so when we recognize that the women mentioned are not the traditionally honored matriarchs. Scholars are not in agreement about why Matthew named Tamar, Rahab, Ruth, "the wife of Uriah" (Bathsheba), and Mary. Some people suggest that what the women have in common is a shady past. That is a hasty conclusion, though, based on a cursory reading of these women's lives. Judah, the son of Isaac, called Tamar "more righteous than I" in her quest for justice (Gen. 38:26). Ruth was repeatedly praised for her strength of character. Bathsheba was forced from her home, violated, and then suffered the death of her husband and first child. The Bible firmly places all of the blame for Bathsheba's trauma on David.[4] Although Rahab was identified as a prostitute, she saved the Hebrew spies from certain death and therefore redeemed herself along with her whole family.

Some suggest that Matthew included the women because they were outsiders who chose to become Israelites. This explanation, while certainly a possibility, does not pertain to Mary, and it does not match the perspective of the rest of Matthew's Gospel. Matthew is not in the habit of suggesting that Gentiles become proselytes before belonging to God's family.

The best explanation for the inclusion of these women in Jesus' genealogy is that these women were tenaciously faithful to God. They were characters who stood outside the normal Israelite narrative and yet took initiative or played a significant role in God's plan.[5] By including these women, therefore, Matthew highlights God's intervention in history through all kinds of people to bring about his purposes. Social traditions do not constrict God: God used the younger son over the older, women along with men, and outsiders along with faithful Israelites. Matthew's edited lineage of Jesus highlights God's faithfulness to his people in the past and hints that God will be faithful to his people through the birth of Jesus. For Matthew, Jesus was Immanuel, "God with us" (Matt. 1:23; 28:20).

While Matthew focuses on Jesus as the Israelite Messiah, Luke retains a more biological emphasis in his crafted lineage.[6] Luke includes many more generations in his list than Matthew does. Instead of working from the earliest ancestor to the most recent (Abraham to Jesus), Luke's list goes from the present to the earliest ancestor (Jesus to Adam). Luke's style mimics the traditional Greco-Roman pattern of genealogies used to portray power, status, and rank. The author uses that style to emphasize the greatness of Jesus.

The placement of the genealogy in Luke's Gospel is also notable. Luke does not explain Jesus' lineage until the middle of chapter 3. Instead of being connected to the birth narrative in chapter 2, Luke uses the genealogy to support statements about Jesus' identity revealed at his baptism (we will discuss this event in the next chapter). When Jesus came out of the water, God said, "You are my Son, whom I love; with you I am well pleased" (Luke 3:22). Luke's genealogy stands as proof of that comment. Instead of stopping with Abraham, as Matthew's list does, the lineage goes all the way back to Adam and then to God. Luke's lineage supports the idea that Jesus was God's Son who was given universal rule over all people and all nations.

The genealogies are good reminders to modern readers that family memories in the biblical text were honored and long lasting. Therefore, when Joseph arrived in Bethlehem and told people he was the son of Jacob, the son of Matthan, who was the son of Eleazar (using Jesus' genealogy record in Matt. 1), he was telling residents of the town how he was connected to Bethlehem and why he should be trusted. He was no outsider. He was family. He had roots in this town. He was known.

Matthew's Narrative

Matthew and Luke agree on the importance of Jesus' birthplace and family roots; but otherwise, the details in their respective birth narratives diverge significantly. Matthew makes bold claims about Jesus' identity and his connection to the Israelite narrative through the genealogy. He then uses ten fulfillment formulas to link Old Testament text to Jesus as the one who fulfills the law and the prophets. Matthew's use of the Old Testament does not mean that Matthew believed that the Israelite prophets *predicted* Jesus' birth. Matthew uses the quotes to prove the continuum of God's fulfilled *promises*.[7]

The difference between *predict* and *promise* initially seems small, but knowing the distinction changes how we perceive Matthew's narrative. A prediction is impersonal and points to an event. For example, I can predict that my students will find fulfilling employment, but that does not imply any kind of commitment on my part to help the prediction come to pass. A promise necessarily involves a personal connection. If I promise my students that they will find fulfilling employment, then a relationship between us is implied. The *me*-and-*you* aspect of the promise matters. I implicate myself in personally contributing to the end goal. A promise *to* my students is different from a prediction *about* my students. Likewise, when Matthew borrows Old Testament quotes, he is not making an impersonal statement about an event that fulfilled a prediction. Matthew chooses quotes connected to the promises God made to his people. God was true to his word at the time of the prophets, and Matthew claims that, in a deeper sense, God fulfilled a greater promise in the personhood of Jesus. Thus we learn more about the character of God and God's intended purpose for his people.

In effect, Matthew says, "This was true then and so too now in Jesus." The full expression of the historical pattern of events, and of God's persistent involvement with his people, comes to a climax in Jesus. In good rabbinic style, Matthew's references prompt us to consider the original context of the quote and reevaluate the story of Jesus in light of the Israelite history. Modern readers, therefore, who may not know the Old Testament as intuitively as Matthew's original audience, need to do a little extra digging.

For example, we find the first Old Testament reference in Matthew 1:19–21 when Joseph did not want to disgrace Mary, so he intended to divorce her quietly. An angel appeared to him and told him not to divorce her, because Mary was pregnant with a son who "will save his people from their sins" (v. 21b). Then Matthew inserts, "All this took place to fulfill what was the Lord had said through the prophet: 'The virgin will conceive and give birth to a son, and they will call him Immanuel'" (a quote from Isa. 7:14). Notice that Matthew does not write, "This is what the prophet said," as if Isaiah predicted Jesus' virgin birth or that his name would be Immanuel. Matthew wrote that this is what God said through the prophet to his people. Matthew wants the reader to explore the promise made by God in the context of Isaiah 7 to discover the larger narrative of which Jesus is a part. Let us pause a moment to understand Isaiah's context.

You may recall from the historical overview chapter that Assyria was a terrifying international threat to the Israelites. Well, during the time of Ahaz, king of Judah, a political partnership between the leaders of the Northern Kingdom of Israel and Syria was as much of a threat to Judah as the one from Assyria. The prophet Isaiah spoke to the king during this time of insecurity, telling him that a child would be born who would be proof of God's presence even in the face of national threats. "For before the boy will know enough to refuse evil and choose good, the land whose two kings you dread will be forsaken" (Isa. 7:16). The life of this child would be a visible sign to the king that God promised to be with his people. The name of the child, Immanuel, means "God with us." Through the prophet Isaiah, God promised to protect Judah from opposing imperial powers. In Isaiah's lifetime, God fulfilled that promise.

Insert that whole context back into Matthew's Gospel. The Jewish people were in a politically perilous situation. Herod the Great was a power-hungry, Rome-loving king. Matthew's use of the Isaiah quote suggests that just as the boy was a sign to Ahaz of God's deliverance against unrighteous powers, so too Jesus was a sign to the Jews of God's faithfulness, even in the face of the Roman Empire. Jesus was Immanuel—the sign of God's presence with his people.

Although Matthew wrote for a Jewish audience, he did not shy away from including details of Gentiles who contributed to the story. Matthew describes the magi from the east who undertook a long journey to visit the child. Who the magi were exactly is a matter of scholarly debate. Details regarding the number of magi, their country of origin, and route they traveled are frustratingly absent from Matthew's text. Some historical writings suggest that the magi were Persians (possibly Parthian), members of the priestly class, and practitioners of astrology, magic, divination, and the interpretation of dreams.[8] They were royal servants, not kings. Historical descriptions of magi fit the magi mentioned in Matthew, but the gifts they brought—gold, frankincense, and myrrh—complicate matters. These goods were typical of the luxury items flowing into the Roman Empire from Arabian spice routes, not from Persia. Therefore, some scholars suggest that these gifts indicate that the magi were Nabatean instead of Persian. This is because the Nabateans controlled the spice trade and governed the land immediately southeast of Roman-controlled lands. During Herod's reign, the Nabateans held a significant amount of territory and proved themselves to be notable rivals. Of course, Persian travelers could have purchased gold, frankincense, and myrrh once they entered Nabatean territory on their way to see Jesus. Basically, we cannot definitively identify the ethnicity of the magi, but we know they were not Roman and that they were from the east.

Matthew's inclusion of the magi in the narrative builds intensity into the scene, while also making political jabs at Herod. Only six decades prior to these events, the Jewish people lost their independence to Rome; and only three decades prior, Herod was appointed king. Herod knew he was strongly disliked by the Jews, who considered him to be an illegitimate ruler. At the time of Jesus' birth, Herod's mental and physical capabilities were deteriorating. You may recall that this was when Herod became increasingly fearful of a usurper and began killing members of his own family.

For a man in Herod's state of mind, hearing of emissaries from the east who wanted to honor the one *born* king was disturbing (Matt. 2:2). Herod spent his early career fighting against the same people who were now in his territory claiming a new and rightful king was born. To make matters worse, Herod was not *born* a king. He was the king *appointed* by the occupying Roman force!

Herod gathered together the chief priests and the scribes. Again, we need to consider the political and religious context. Ever since Pompey entered Jerusalem, Rome controlled who filled priestly positions, so the chief priests were Herod's allies—members of the ruling class based at the Jerusalem temple. They were well versed in the Hebrew Scriptures and told Herod of the Micah tradition that stated, "Out of you will come for me one who will be ruler over Israel" (Mic. 5:2). Remember, Bethlehem's size was unimpressive, but it preserved the memory of Israel's great King David. As Matthew retells the narrative, he specifically includes the quote from Micah to connect Jesus to the promised descendent of David who would be the Jewish Messiah (Matt. 2:5–6).

The contrast between the responses to Jesus' birth from the magi and from Herod is notable. They both represent Gentiles who are in positions of power. The magi came to worship the king of the Jews, and they did this with joy and generous offerings. Specifying what their offerings were may have reminded Matthew's audience of Isaiah 60 and Psalm 72—texts that promise that the coming Messiah will cause the Gentiles to bring gifts and to acknowledge God's reign in Zion. In contrast, Herod reacted out of suspicion. The visit from the magi intensified Herod's fears of losing control, prompting a vicious command to kill all the young boys in Bethlehem. Herod sacrificed innocent lives to protect his position of power.

Matthew says that an angel warned Joseph to leave Bethlehem, so Joseph took his young family to Egypt. Matthew inserts another Old Testament fulfillment quote here: "And so was fulfilled what the Lord had said through the prophet: 'Out of Egypt I called my son'" (Hos. 11:1; cf. Matt. 2:15). Again, Matthew is not claiming that Hosea *predicted* that Jesus would live in Egypt as a child. After all, Hosea 11 is a look backward at past events when God brought his son Israel (Exod. 4:22; Deut. 1:31) out of the oppression of Egypt. Matthew uses the context of Hosea to place Jesus in the continued Israelite narrative as a fulfilled *promise*. Just as God brought Israel "his son" out of Egypt, so too God brought Jesus, "his son," out of Egypt. This quote encourages Matthew's readers to look at the rest of the Gospel with these questions in mind: Will Jesus be a perfect Israelite? Will he face the same challenges and succeed where the Israelites failed?

Geography also contributes layers of meaning to the narrative. The magi arrive from the east, and then Joseph's family makes a brief journey into Egypt before returning to Nazareth. Such details touch on geographical themes from the Israelite narrative. Abraham was called out of Mesopotamia to the land God would specify. Jacob's family sought shelter in Egypt, and then God brought the Israelites out of Egypt and gave them their land. All of Israelite history is centered on this small piece of land. The place of these events reinforces that Jesus' birth narrative is contextualized in the wider Gentile world but with deep roots in the land of Israelite history. As mentioned in an earlier chapter, this land was not a world-*dominating* place but a world-*influencing* place. If Jesus was the Messiah, then his actions would impact surrounding people.

Luke's Narrative

Like Matthew's Gospel, the details in Luke's text reflect a culture from a time and a place different from our own. Luke assumes that his audience understood the Roman census, structure of homes, and the agricultural calendar. When modern readers miss the significance of these cultural clues, the story ends up being interpreted through our cultural norms instead of Luke's. This is how we end up with a grumpy innkeeper, a donkey, and a very pregnant Mary.

Luke attributes the reason for Mary and Joseph's journey to the census that Caesar Augustus required of the "entire Roman world" (Luke 2:1).[9] A follow-up explanation tells the reader that this was the same census taken while Quirinius was governor of Syria (v. 2). A quick review of history makes this statement confusing.

From the early days of the Roman Republic, a national register was maintained of those eligible for military service; it was also used to establish taxation policies. The census was discontinued only to be revived again by Augustus, who used it as a system to establish provincial rule and to create tribute lists. The function of the census changed from recording military service to extracting taxes from the people whom Rome had conquered. There is no historical evidence that a census was taken throughout the entire Roman world.

To further complicate matters, Herod died around 4 BCE, which was about the time when Jesus was born. Herod was the vassal king for Rome. He collected his own taxes to send to Rome, so a census was not necessary until sometime after his death. The Quirinius mentioned in Luke's Gospel did rule Syria, and he did manage a local census, but that was in 6–7 CE, which was about ten years *after* the birth of Jesus. Quirinius oversaw the census conducted after Herod's son Archelaus was exiled to Gaul.

The discrepancy in Luke is not easy to explain. Certainly, Herod taxed the people. But after Herod's death, Rome leveraged a new and oppressive form of taxation. Rioting as a form of protest against Rome was common in the time following Herod's death. Perhaps Luke conflated the chaotic final year of Herod's rule with the uncertainty of the times surrounding the census in 6 CE. What is certain, however, is that Jesus was born into a politically charged and contentious environment.

Luke says that Mary and Joseph traveled from Galilee to Bethlehem—about a seventy- or ninety-mile journey depending on the route.[10] Many Christmas scenes depict a very pregnant Mary riding on a donkey, but she probably walked. How do we know? Luke 2:22–24 says that after the birth of Jesus, Mary and Joseph went to the temple in Jerusalem to fulfill the command to dedicate the firstborn child to the Lord. According to Leviticus 12, new parents must offer a one-year-old lamb for a burnt offering or two turtledoves if they cannot afford the lamb. Mary and Joseph offered two doves as a sacrifice at Jesus' circumcision. The young couple was evidently poor, which makes it unlikely that they owned a donkey. It is also unlikely that Mary was nine months pregnant when they walked to Bethlehem. Knowing the journey would take five to seven days, Mary and Joseph probably traveled earlier in the pregnancy to prevent giving birth along the way.

When the couple arrived in Bethlehem, where did they stay? Remember, Bethlehem was a small town. Although in our minds, we think of Mary and Joseph searching for accommodations at an inn, such a picture does not do the narrative justice, nor is it a proper reflection of ancient village culture.

Although a network of inns that housed travelers did exist along Roman roads, the Greek word for those inns is *pandocheion*, which is the same word Luke uses later in the parable of the Good Samaritan (Luke 10:34). However, those kinds of accommodations were not available everywhere. They existed primarily along Roman roads, not in the small towns. When Luke describes Joseph and Mary in Bethlehem, he does not use the word *pandocheion* to refer to their housing. He uses the word *kataluma*, better translated as "guest room" or "spare room." This is the same word Luke uses to describe the spare room of someone's house where Jesus and the disciples shared a final meal (Luke 22:11).

Village life functioned on deeply imbedded cultural expectations of hospitality. Travelers were invited into family homes and came under the protection of that family. The *kataluma* was where travelers stayed to rest while they replenished supplies. Joseph traveled to Bethlehem because his ancestors were from there. The cultural assumption was that a local family would host them. Maybe Joseph still had family living in Bethlehem, in which case, he would have stayed with them.

To understand the context even further, we need to explore the layout of the home. At least three generations would have lived together in one home—the parents, their children, and perhaps the father's elderly parents. Many homes had two floors built around a common area. In the larger homes, brothers had separate rooms for their families, but the extended family shared a common courtyard and kitchen. The rooms farthest from the entrance were the private rooms where valuable tools or family commodities and food supplies were kept. The family slept on the second floor, where there was an additional room available to guests—the *kataluma*. Daily social activities, like grinding grain or baking bread, and public events, parties, and celebrations took place in the courtyard or in the front of the house closer to the street.[11] Also on the ground floor, or possibly in a cave below the house, was a room where the animals owned by the family were brought during times of danger or in inclement weather. In Bethlehem, families engaged in both farming and shepherding vocations. Housing the animals inside was practical, especially in the rainy season when prolonged exposure to the damp cold created a high probability of the animals becoming sick. Giving shelter to the animals preserved their health and thus protected the family fortune. The added bonus was that the body heat from the animals warmed the house. However, during the dry season when the sun was relentlessly hot, keeping the animals outside and under the watchful eye of shepherds was more pleasant for animals and people alike.

Luke 2:7 says that Mary wrapped Jesus in cloth and placed him in a manger because there was no room for them in the *kataluma*. Exactly why the host family was unable to place them in the *kataluma* is open for speculation. Maybe other members of Joseph's extended family arrived in Bethlehem prior to Mary and Joseph, so the guest room was full. Instead of turning the young couple away, their hosts gave them the room on the lower level of the house where the animals normally stayed.

Luke's Gospel also says that "while they were there, the time came for the baby to be born" (2:6). This implies that there is a gap of time between when the couple arrived and when Mary gave birth. Would the town have shunned this young couple? We emphasize the shame of an unwed, pregnant girl, but this betrays a faulty recognition of betrothal. Mary and Joseph had a binding contract to be married. They were waiting for Joseph to build the rooms where they would stay once married. Sexual intercourse between betrothal and marriage ceremony did not violate any norm. The truly shocking part in the narrative is that Mary was pregnant and Joseph knew he was not the father. He had grounds to divorce her for assumed sexual relations with another man. Instead, Joseph chose to stay with Mary, and thus everyone would assume Joseph was the father of Jesus.[12] Even so, the circumstances around her pregnancy would not trump the ingrained cultural rules to care for a pregnant woman. Childbirth was dangerous, and the life of the mother and the child were at risk. Most likely, the room was cleared of men, the village midwife beckoned, and women from the house stood by to assist. When it was time for Jesus to be born, Mary was in the room where animals were typically kept because there was no room in the normal guest room. There was space downstairs because the animals were outside with the shepherds. The culturally correct picture we should have in our minds is of Mary giving birth in a house with many knowledgeable women around to help. The young couple were not on their own to deliver their first baby.

Luke says that Mary gave birth in the room where animals were typically housed, because the shepherds were "living out in the fields nearby, keeping watch over their flocks at night" (2:8). Remember the description of the agricultural calendar in chapter 2? (See Figure 3 on page 36 to refresh your memory!) There were two seasons, dry and wet, and the earliest crops harvested were the grains. After the harvest, shepherds took flocks into the fields to eat the stubble and fertilize the fields. If the sheep were in the agricultural fields, as Luke describes, we can assume these events took place, at the *earliest*, after the wheat harvest at the end of May or early June.[13] The fact that the shepherds and sheep were outside at night suggests that the evening air was nicer than being cooped up inside. These events had to take place in the dry season, after the grain harvest, but before the farmer prepared the fields for the next agricultural cycle. Most likely, Jesus was born in Bethlehem sometime between July and September. We joke about having "Christmas in July," but this is actually more accurate than December!

The shepherds in the field were a humble audience for the angelic announcement of the birth of a child. "Today in the town of David a Savior has been born to you; he is the Messiah, the Lord" (Luke 2:11). Notice that the angel does not say Bethlehem but identifies the connection back to David and to the hoped-for royal descendent. David was a shepherd in his youth, and now these shepherds witnessed the arrival of his royal descendant. Three specific titles are used in the declaration of Jesus' birth: Savior, Messiah, and Lord. Messiah (or "Christ" in Greek) was a Hebrew title for the anointed one of God. Although kings, prophets, and priests could be anointed of God, the combined titles of "Messiah Lord" referred to the expected royal Messiah. The terms "Savior" and "Lord" were common epithets for Roman emperors.[14] In one sentence, Jesus is identified as the descendent of David, the expected Messiah, and the one deserving more honor than the Roman Caesar. It must have been remarkable for common shepherds to receive such a grand announcement, only to find the child in a regular home like their own.

Conclusion

Matthew and Luke put their unique spins on the awesomeness of Jesus' birth. Matthew helps readers recognize Jesus' connection to the Israelite narrative. He emphasizes Jesus' role as the continued fulfillment of the promises God gave his people many years before. Jesus was Immanuel, "God with us," the child who would change the world. A tremendous sense of anticipation builds around Jesus' role in the continuation of the story.

Luke gives the reader a personal, albeit gritty, look at Jesus' birth. Understanding the cultural norms of the day uncovers a different picture from the modern wintery, Christmas scene of peaceful and quiet isolation. Jesus was not a rejected Messiah born on a cold night. In fact, the whole birth narrative is about people welcoming Jesus with wonder and accepting him into a loud, messy family. It is comforting to recognize that Jesus was born into the middle of real life and a real community.

7

ENTERING MINISTRY

We learned in the last chapter that Matthew and Luke gave readers detailed descriptions of Jesus' birth, hinting at the significance of Jesus' life within the whole story of Israel. They told us about Mary and Joseph taking Jesus to Egypt to flee Herod's wrath; and when the family returned and heard that Herod's son Archelaus was in charge of Judea, they relocated to Nazareth in Galilee, where Herod Antipas was in charge (Matt. 2:22). Then the details of Jesus' childhood dry up, and we are left with almost no stories. We assume Jesus had a traditional, Jewish upbringing in a small village that had limited natural resources. He grew up with brothers and sisters (Matt. 13:55–56; Mark 6:3), went to school with other children to memorize the Torah and the oral teachings of the rabbis (as evidenced in Luke 2:41–52), and learned a practical trade from Joseph.

As discussed in chapter 2, Nazareth's location surrounded Jesus with a landscape that preserved many Israelite stories, thus anchoring him in a rich heritage. Everyone in Nazareth relied on subsistence living, so Jesus was familiar with the lived realities of the land—weather patterns, crops, flowers, animals—information that would enhance how he taught crowds of land-oriented people in later years (which we will discuss in the next chapter). We can assume that sometime during those growing-up years, Jesus learned about his special relationship with God and thought deeply about himself, his people, and his calling in life.[1]

While Nazareth provided a safe environment for Jesus' childhood years, the village was not a large enough context for his public ministry. The same elements that created a safe environment were also a hinderance to the spread of Jesus' message. How does a man move from obscurity in a small village onto the public stage? According to the Gospels, this point of transition happened with Jesus' baptism, after which he made waves with his teachings and, from the view of Jewish leaders, chose all the wrong people to be his disciples. Let us take this step by step, as we look at the identity of Jesus, the goal of his mission, and the radical nature of his community.

The Forerunner

The Gospel writers introduce Jesus' public ministry by first introducing readers to his fascinating relative, John the Baptist. Matthew and Mark specifically describe John as a man who wore a garment of camel's hair and a leather belt, and who ate locust and wild honey (Matt. 3:4; Mark 1:6). These details are not as random as they may first appear. They connect John to one of Israel's great prophets, Elijah, who is described in 2 Kings 1:8 as a hairy man with a leather belt around his waist. By associating John's physical appearance with that of Elijah's, Matthew and Mark hint to their readers that John was the Elijah-type figure, preparing the way for the coming Messiah as promised in the book of Malachi (Mal. 4:5–6).

All four of the Gospels describe John as "the voice of one crying in the wilderness." The phrase refers to a well-known passage from Isaiah 40, in which a figure announces the end of Israel's exile and rejoices in the restoration of God's kingdom in Jerusalem. The Gospel writers appropriate this prophecy to characterize John as the forerunner to the Messiah, and also to tell the readers that in the coming narrative, Jesus will be the fulfillment of God's kingdom established in Jerusalem.

John stirred the crowds to repent, proclaiming that the Day of the Lord, the day of divine judgment, had arrived. For those whose lives bore the fruit of repentance, though, God's long-awaited restoration was upon them. John did not mince words, and his message called his audience to live radically changed lives. Despite this challenging message, the people were intrigued enough to leave their cities and towns to see this preacher-man in the wilderness.

To modern readers, John's characterization may seem unusual, but his Jewish audience would have noticed the similarities between him and the Essenes, a group that removed themselves from what they perceived to be an unscrupulous society. They spoke against the corruption in the temple, and they considered themselves to be the true remnant of Israel through whom God would restore his kingdom. Being the remnant, of course, required an attitude of repentance and a lifestyle of purity. Their writings convey the practice of immersion in water to ritually clean the body, but only if the soul was already purified through righteous behavior. Although historical evidence does not suggest that John joined the Essenes, his lifestyle and message were similar to that of the Essene community.

John understood baptism as evidence of repentance. He told the crowds that no one entered the water unless they repented of evil and had a lifestyle in line with Torah (justice toward one another and piety toward God).[2] John was an intriguing figure. Crowds followed him. Disciples followed him. But John knew he was paving the way for someone else.

Jesus sought out John near the water and asked to be baptized by him. Jesus had no need of personal repentance, but he identified himself with those who expressed their longing to be right with God.[3] This one event, as told to us by the Gospel writers, is layered with symbolism. Not only did Jesus acknowledge John's ministry by seeking to be baptized by him, but Jesus also saw his own life as the fulfillment of Scripture's promises of restoration. To clarify the significance in this event, we need to look at the geography, symbolic pictures, and quoted Scripture in this narrative.

Geography, Symbolism, and Scripture

Pinpointing the exact location where Jesus was baptized is not possible, but textual clues help scholars make an educated guess about the general region. The Gospel of Matthew places John in the "wilderness of Judea" (3:1), which is on the eastern side of the hill country. Mark simply says "wilderness" (1:4) but also mentions the Jordan River (v. 5), which means we can narrow down the area to the wilderness north of the Dead Sea. Luke writes that John was in the "country around the Jordan" (3:3), leaving the whole length of the Jordan River in question. The Gospel of John mentions "Bethany on the other side of the Jordan" (1:28). The phrase "the other side of the Jordan" referred to the eastern side of the river where there were more roads, villages, and travelers due to the availability of food and water. The ancient site of Bethany is challenging to locate today, but Christian tradition preserves its memory east of Jericho. Using the given geographical clues, it is sensible to conclude that on the day Jesus chose to be baptized, John was near the Jordan River to the east of wilderness surrounding Jericho. This location makes the narrative even more interesting, because of the memory of significant events from Israel's past that occurred in this place.

Figure 19. Jordan River (photo by author).

It was on the eastern shore of the Jordan River opposite Jericho that Moses laid hands on Joshua and anointed him the new leader of the Israelites. Following Joshua's instructions, the Israelites then passed through the waters, from east to west, and entered their land of inheritance. Joshua began a new career as a military leader, and the Israelites began a new life as settled, instead of nomadic, people (Deut. 31; Josh. 3).

Toward the end of the prophet Elijah's ministry, he and his disciple, Elisha, briefly stopped in Jericho before walking to the Jordan River. At the edge of the river, Elijah took off his cloak and hit the river. The waters separated, and the mentor and his protégé passed through. Elisha then requested a double portion of Elijah's spirit. After seeing the vision of Elijah ascending to heaven, Elisha picked up Elijah's cloak and used it to hit the Jordan River. The waters parted, just as they had for Elijah, and Elisha crossed through the river, from east to west, and began his prophetic career (2 Kings 2).

Before Jesus' baptism, John was the primary figure people went out to see and listen to, but now the focus shifted to Jesus. The pattern from the earlier Israelite stories repeats in this narrative when the primary mantle of leadership passed from one figure to the next on the eastern shoreline of the river. To the careful reader, this specific event in this location indicates a massive shift in the narrative. John is no longer the primary character; Jesus is, and he is about to start something new.

Seeing Meaning in Patterns

Jesus belongs to a larger Israelite narrative. Pictures and patterns are important aspects of Jewish storytelling, so modern readers must train their eyes to see the pattern of images; in this case, the water images. Think of all the Israelite stories that involved separating waters (we talked about many of these in chapter 1). We can start "in the beginning" with creation where Genesis 1 describes the Spirit of God fluttering over the chaotic waters and how God split the chaos, forming a new and beautiful creation.

In the flood story, the waters from above and from below crashed in on themselves and obliterated life. Noah sent out birds from the ark that flew over the waters, which is reminiscent of God's Spirit fluttering over the waters in the creation story. Dry ground appeared, and a new life was possible for Noah's descendants (Gen. 6–8).

Think of the exodus when God brought the Israelites out of the chaotic oppression of Egypt. When the people became trapped at the edge of the Sea of Reeds,[4] God sent an eastern wind to divide the waters. Israel then passed through on dry ground and entered the Sinai, where God formed them into a new nation (Exod. 14–15). Forty years later, when the nation of Israel left the wilderness, God split the Jordan River and the people crossed on dry ground to enter their land of inheritance (Josh. 3).

Each narrative contains water (often symbolic of danger and chaos), God's presence, and God's Spirit or wind. Dividing and calming the chaotic waters marked the beginning of something new. Now let's bring these images and patterns to Jesus' baptism. The Gospels of Matthew, Mark, and Luke state that immediately after coming up out of the water, Jesus saw the heavens open and the Spirit of God descend in the form of a dove. Water, God's presence, and his Spirit, in the form of a dove, are all present. The Gospel writers have added here another layer to the picture of Jesus, which signals to the reader that a new era is about to begin with Jesus.

The geography and the pattern of images are not the only provocative details here. For after the baptism, a voice from heaven said, "You are my Son, whom I love; with you I am well pleased" (Mark 1:11; cf. Matt. 3:17). These words are an amalgamation of two or three quotes from the Hebrew Scriptures. "You are my son" is taken from Psalm 2:7, which is an enthronement psalm of a Davidic king that was likely sung during coronation ceremonies. The song declares that the king is a legitimate ruler with God-given authority. Inserting "whom I love" may possibly echo the events recorded in Genesis 22 in which God asked Abraham to sacrifice his son, his only son, his beloved son Isaac. God stopped the hand of Abraham, but the reader should wonder if God would spare his own "beloved son" from future harm. The quote from Psalm 2, with the modification from Genesis 22, embeds the regal title with undertones of patriarchal faith. "With you I am well pleased" is a reference to the beginning of Isaiah 42. This chapter is a part of a larger collection of servant songs that start with kingly imagery and then describe the redemption of God's people through God's chosen servant. This single declaration that Jesus heard when he came out of the water described his identity and his mission. Jesus had a special relationship with God and was being granted the authority of the Davidic king for the divine purpose of restoration.[5]

In the previous chapter, we noted that Luke's Gospel inserted Jesus' genealogy at this point in the narrative. The genealogy presents a contrast between who people thought Jesus was (the son of Joseph) and the true identity of Jesus as God's son. The Gospel writers let their audience question what it meant for Jesus to be called the Son of God, given the knowledge that Israel was considered God's son. What did the Israelites fail to do that Jesus, as God's son, would do as a representative of God's people?

Temptation in the Wilderness

Since the Gospels are creating parallels between the beginning of Jesus' ministry and the beginning of the Israelite nation, let us pause here to consider the progression of the Israelite narrative from Egypt to their land of inheritance. The people fled the oppression of Egypt, passed through the Sea of Reeds, and became a new nation at the base of Mount Sinai. But in the harsh wilderness, the Israelites grumbled among themselves, wondering if they had left Egypt only to die in the Sinai wilderness. The wounds of their oppression were too fresh, and they doubted the goodness of God to provide for them in such a destitute land. Their second-guessing and complaining resulted in forty years of wandering through this wilderness.

Figure 21. Overlooking the Judean Wilderness (photo by author).

In the Gospels, we have seen that Jesus passed through waters in his baptism, followed immediately by God's Spirit leading Jesus out into the wilderness for forty days. If, as the Gospel writers suggest, Jesus took on a representative role for all of Israel, then how would he respond to being in a destitute land? How would his reaction be any different from the Israelites' reaction during their time in the wilderness? If Jesus took on the identity of Israel, he also had to take on the responsibility of Israel. He had to live as God wanted Israel to live.

Although we are not given details about what Jesus did during those forty days, we do know that at the end he faced three significant temptations. Jesus had the Scriptures memorized, and since he responded to each temptation with passages from Deuteronomy, then maybe he spent forty days literally doing what Deuteronomy says, "Remember!"[6] Deuteronomy is the book that reminds the Israelites of God's actions in the past and of their identity as God's people. It teaches the people how to live a life that is completely oriented to God through their values, priorities, actions, and relationships. Let us therefore use the context of Deuteronomy to help examine Jesus' responses to the temptations.

At the end of forty days, the tempter tried three times to convince Jesus to compromise God's plans. The first temptation challenged Jesus' identity, and this temptation has two elements. The first part is when the tempter says, "If you are the Son of God . . . " Questioning the goodness and faithfulness of God is easy to do when surrounded by barren and parched ground, which is exactly what the Israelites did in the Sinai wilderness. Would God truly lead his son into such a hard place? Would Jesus, like the Israelites before him, doubt his identity because of his circumstances? If not, then the second part of the temptation challenged Jesus' willingness to be vulnerable before God: "Turn these stones into bread." The temptation now is not one of capability but of trust. Turning stones into bread was not out of reach for Jesus, but would he rely on himself or his father to provide? Jesus responded with a quote from Deuteronomy 8—a chapter that reminded the Israelites that their survival in the wilderness was due to God's provision. Jesus answered, "Man shall not live on bread alone, but on every word that comes from the mouth of God." When tempted to provide for himself instead of depending on God, Jesus declared his confidence that God was trustworthy.

The second temptation[7] shifted the action away from the wilderness to the pinnacle of the temple in Jerusalem. The tempter told Jesus to jump, for surely God would intervene and protect his chosen one from striking his "foot against a stone" (the tempter himself manipulating the meaning of Psalm 91). In other words, the tempter suggested that in the most public place in the city, Jesus should make a grandiose and miraculous appearance as the long-awaited Messiah. This temptation was not for Jesus to refuse the mission of Messiah but to create a spectacular role as Messiah. Again, Jesus responded with a quote from Deuteronomy: "Do not put the Lord your God to the test" (Deut. 6:16). Jesus left unspoken the rest of the sentence, which is "as you did at Massah." Massah was the place in the wilderness where the people grumbled and doubted God. Jesus stated that he would not test God's faithfulness, but instead he embodied Deuteronomy's instructions to trust God.

The final temptation involved kingdom-building and power. The tempter suggested that with one simple act of bowing down and worshiping him, Jesus could have all the kingdoms of the world. If Jesus was God's chosen one with the authority of the Davidic king to bring about the divine purpose of restoration, then why shouldn't he take the easy path to the final goal? Why travel the slow road through years of misunderstandings and pain, when Jesus could be the ruler of nations in an instant? Jesus' statement "Love the Lord your God and serve him only" was a reaffirmation of what was at the heart of Deuteronomy 6, and indeed all Israelite identity. There is only one God, and Jesus worshiped and obeyed him only. There were no short-cuts to establishing God's kingdom.

First, Jesus passed through the waters and received an identity and a purpose for his ministry; and second, the Holy Spirit led him into the wilderness, where he resisted temptation and embodied Deuteronomy's commands to love God only. Based on the strong parallels between Israel's story and Jesus' life, the reader can anticipate the next stage of Jesus' ministry. After the Israelite wilderness wanderings came the kingdom building, and after Jesus' time in the wilderness, he began to draw people into conversations about God's kingdom. Who was welcomed in the kingdom, and what did restoration look like? Indeed, the restoration Jesus talked about was imminent, but not in the way the Jews anticipated. They looked back to David's kingdom as the example for restoration and to the temple as the example of God's presence in the midst of his people. Jesus looked back to creation and the necessity of fixing the underlying brokenness between God and humanity and nature. As Israel's representative, Jesus began his mission to bring about God's restoration. Perhaps you can see how with two different ideas about what "kingdom" meant, Jesus had the challenge to reshape the people's understanding of what God was doing.

Calling a Motley Crew of Disciples

You will recall from chapter 5 that the Jewish people highly valued education. They instituted a system to educate their children in the local synagogue, and a few brilliant students had opportunities to look for a rabbi to follow. Jesus broke all the social norms. He went out and called young men who were already working in the family business, meaning they were not among the "few brilliant students." The men Jesus chose had a basic education that included memorizing the Torah; but at some point, their best option had been to leave full-time study and learn the family trade. The invitation from a rabbi—even this radical, social-norm-breaking rabbi—to become a disciple was an honor and a once-in-a-lifetime opportunity. However, choosing unlikely disciples from unexpected places was the equivalent of a red flag in the eyes of some scholars.

A quick look at the list of Jesus' twelve disciples suggests that he sought out a diverse group (cf. Matt. 10:2–4). There were two sets of brothers, Peter and Andrew as well as James and John. They, along with Philip and Bartholomew, were fishermen. Then there were Thomas, James, and Thaddaeus, about whom not much is known. Of course, there was Judas Iscariot, who would later betray Jesus. Matthew was a tax collector and a cog in the great Roman wheel, while Simon was a Zealot who grew up with the rebellious ideology of undermining Roman power. In all the long hours these guys spent with Jesus, how do you think Matthew and Simon got along? What about the discrepancies in economic status among the disciples? We assume most of them grew up in Galilee, where the open valleys and international roads led to familiarity with a broad exchange of ideas. Some scholars guess that Judas may have come from Judean Hills, where the geography created more conservative communities. Even if they all came from Jewish families, their experiences in life were different. We are not told about interpersonal dynamics between the disciples, but they must have had debates with one another as they followed Jesus from place to place.

Jesus' teachings and his views of being the Messiah were not easily understood by the disciples. Even though they followed Jesus, ate with him, and probed the meaning of his words, it took time for them to fully transform their thoughts about how he would bring restoration. When they did accept that Jesus was the Messiah, Jesus immediately began to teach them of his impending death and resurrection. But we get ahead of ourselves. We are still at the beginning.

As Jesus moved into his public ministry, he shifted his home base from the conservative Jewish village of Nazareth to the bustling city of Capernaum.[8] The diverse residents of Capernaum included farmers, fishermen, soldiers, tax collectors, and religious leaders. According to the Gospels, Jesus spent much of his time around the shoreline of the Sea of Galilee where the three political divisions of Galilee, Gaulanitis, and Decapolis converged. Relocating to Capernaum opened possibilities of interacting with diverse people in diverse occupations. This was a perfect spot for Jesus to train his disciples on how to interact with people, and the surrounding hills provided optimal gathering places for the crowds.

Jesus' actions were unorthodox, and some leaders likely thought he was heretical. Jesus had a unique interpretation of Torah and chose the most unlikely people to learn, memorize, and absorb his message. Disagreements about proper Torah interpretation, however, were not new. After all, a variety of prominent Jewish sects already existed—Sadducees, Pharisees, and Essenes—and a new group of Zealots were branching off from the Pharisees. There was a multitude of rabbis with different opinions on how to interpret the Torah for their current society. So, Jesus fit in this time and place, even though he was introducing something new and using a strange collection of disciples to do it. Do you think you would have been suspicious of such a rabbi?

Conclusion

With his baptism, Jesus took on a dangerous calling. People longed for the Messiah, but they had a different understanding of what the Messiah's role would be. The crowds wanted a human leader who could unify them and lead them in a revolt against Rome, so they assumed God would use the Messiah to overthrow foreign powers and set up God's kingdom on earth with a human king. Jesus did not disassociate himself from the Jewish hope of restoration. The question was not *that* restoration should happen but *how* it would happen and what it would mean.[9] Jesus had to be a brilliant teacher to communicate his idea of Messiah before the people became too excited and forced him into the political role of king. In the next chapter, we will discuss how Jesus used land images, politics, and fables to communicate effectively with the diverse population around the Sea of Galilee and to convey his vision for the role of the Messiah.

8

A Skilled Communicator

Chapter 5 introduced us to the wide variety of people in Jewish society. We need to keep in mind that in Jesus' public ministry, he interacted with everyone from the Jewish elite to the hard-working farmers, and from Roman citizens to Jewish peasants. Jesus taught in people's homes, on open hill sides, in the synagogues, and in the temple courts, varying his teaching method depending on where he was and with whom he was speaking. As a skilled communicator, he used everything from technical speech to parables and popular fables to resonate with the cultural reality of the audience.

On a few occasions, Jesus was in Jerusalem where he interacted with the Jewish elite, who were at the top of the social pyramid and experienced the luxurious lifestyles modeled after Roman norms. This group included the Hasmoneans and the Sadducees, who were some of Jesus' harshest critics. Once we recognize the context and the history associated with the people who had positions of power in the temple and connections with political influencers, their harsh critiques of Jesus make more sense. Not to say that his critics were correct, but we can better understand the concerns of those worried about their financial and political stability. They had a lot to lose if a new messianic figure gathered crowds of people, claimed God's kingdom had arrived, and instigated a revolt against the Roman Empire.

Whether Jesus was in Jerusalem or traveling through the countryside, the Gospels record his technical debates with the scribes, Pharisees, and experts in the law. These conversations were heated enough that modern audiences who read these Gospel accounts often conclude that the Pharisees were nasty people always in conflict with Jesus. We forget that the Pharisees argued with Jesus because they loved the Torah and desired to honor God. They were simply not convinced that Jesus' unique interpretations of Scripture were the right ones. And remember that for those who had a Jewish education, debates were expected and disagreements were not a sign of animosity. Without being familiar with the underlying technicality of the debates in the first century, it is easy to brush aside Jesus' opponents as overly antagonistic. Such conclusions dismiss the reality of Jesus' time and undercut the true love Pharisees had for the Torah.

If we follow Jesus' travels on a map, we notice that he and the disciples walked near many large urban areas, such as Sepphoris (five miles from his hometown of Nazareth) and Tiberius (along the shoreline of the Sea of Galilee). With all the travel between Galilee and the city of Jerusalem, Jesus certainly walked by the massive Decapolis city of Scythopolis. These large cities, however, were not his primary place for teaching. In fact, given the economic and cultural significance of urban areas in the first century, cities are surprisingly absent from the Gospels. The narratives focus instead on Jesus in villages or out in nature where large crowds of common people gathered outside city walls.

Jesus' audience is often referred to as "the crowd," which makes them seem like a faceless, singular entity. When we read that Jesus taught "the crowd," who exactly were these people? Based on what you already know of Jewish society, how do you picture them? Jesus' twelve disciples followed him, but so too did several women (Luke 8:2–3). There were a small number of the wealthy elite, such as Zacchaeus (Luke 19) or the rich young ruler (Matt. 19:16), who found Jesus to be fascinating. The largest numbers in the crowd were most likely the commoners, and those socially estranged or marginalized—the destitute, sick, landless, poor. When we think of the crowds who listened to Jesus, we should think of plurality and recognize that there was always an undercurrent of revolution, as many of the Jewish people longed for political independence once again.

Dynamic Communication

We have established that Jesus engaged religious leaders with technical debates about Torah. But with the crowds, Jesus used a variety of teaching methods such as fables, land illustrations, political events, and parables to communicate effectively to a broad range of people with a broad range of concerns. Jesus used language that was dynamic, colorful, and action centered. He captured their attention, aroused their curiosity, and used questions to get people to think and engage. Some people responded with interest, while others were enraged.

When asked to explain himself, Jesus did not go through the logical reasoning of why he made sense as the Jewish Messiah (that would be a Western mind-set approach!). Instead, he engaged people with stories. To explain abstract concepts such as forgiveness and repentance, he provided concrete realities from the land. In response to what God's kingdom was like, Jesus used analogies based on the crowd's experiences in real life, giving the kingdom of God rooted and earthly qualities.

Nature and Weather

Before discussing how Jesus taught using land images, let us remember the basics about that particular land. The inhabitable places where the Gospel stories happened were sandwiched between the influences of Mediterranean Sea and the Arabian desert. The land relied on the western breeze to bring the rain clouds, and people collected water in the rainy season and rationed this precious commodity throughout the dry season. Eastern winds from the desert arrived during transition times between the rainy and dry seasons, bringing fine sand particles mixed with scorching hot winds. The air turned a sepia color, and for the few days it lasted, the eastern wind had a desiccating effect on nature.

Now think about a short interaction between Jesus and the crowd: "See how the flowers of the field grow. They do not labor or spin" (Matt. 6:28; Luke 12:27).[1] Well, what would the crowd have known about lilies (as these flowers are called in some translations)? They likely knew that lilies needed a large amount of rain to grow and that they appeared in a broad range of vivid colors. Jesus said these simple flowers were more luxurious than anything Solomon had. But the people also knew that the flowers flourished for only a short time before the eastern winds brought the heat of dry season that scorched the earth. If God extravagantly clothed these short-lived lilies, would he not be as extravagant in his provision for his people?

Luke records another version of Jesus' use of weather patterns. Jesus commended the crowds on their ability to understand the natural signs: a cloud from the west that brought rain, and a wind from the south that scorched the earth (Luke 12:54; similar teachings in Matt. 16:1–4). But Jesus went on to rebuke them for not accurately understanding the events of the day. To what was Jesus referring?[2] There may be a possible allusion here to the covenant between God and his people. There is a pattern throughout Scripture of the ideal garden-like context in which the relationship between God and humans and nature is restored. Deuteronomy declares that when the people stay true to their covenant with God, then God brings the early and the late rains that guarantee a successful annual harvest (Deut. 11:13–15). But the consequences for a broken covenant were lack of rain, increase in pestilence, and famine (Deut. 28:21–24). These were warning signs that the people had turned away from God. The natural world thus proclaimed the health or the brokenness of the covenant. Jesus told the crowd that if they correctly interpreted the weather patterns for the day's activities, then why could they not see the larger picture? Jesus taught about a restored covenant and a new creation, and he prodded his audience to stretch their understanding and grasp the implications of his teachings.

Villages and Cities

Understanding where Jesus taught is as important for interpreting Jesus' teachings as understanding the physical land. Take, for instance, the Sermon on the Mount (Matt. 5–7). While there is a modern church on a sloping hill on the north side of the Sea of Galilee (see Figure 15 on page 62 for the map of this area) that commemorates this event, identifying the precise place where Jesus taught this sermon is impossible. But the exact hill almost does not matter, for all of the hills provide a commanding view of the area around the Sea of Galilee. Even today, it is possible to read this sermon as you stand on a hillside and gaze around to see what was on the immediate horizon line for the listening crowds.

Along the northwestern shoreline sat the bustling Jewish town of Magdala. Excavations show that it had a large harbor and shops near the harbor with catchment basins to hold the fresh fish the fishermen hauled onto shore. Magdala created a large industry out of salting and preserving fish. In the sermon, Jesus said, "You are the salt of the earth," and I always imagine a simple hand gesture toward Magdala. "But if the salt loses its saltiness, how can it be made salty again?" (Matt. 5:13). Jesus borrowed from the crowd's immediate context to bring home the implications of them being a witness to the world.

Similarly, on the horizon—but on the other side of the lake and perched on a prominent hill—was the large Decapolis city of Hippos. This city represented the glory of Rome, and like any modern urban skyline at night, the light shining from Hippos would have been visible to everyone around the lake. Jesus told the crowd, "You are the light of the world. A town built on a hill cannot be hidden." I imagine the crowd's eyes involuntarily glancing toward Hippos. "Let your light shine before others, that they may see your good deeds and glorify your Father in heaven" (Matt 5:14, 16). What a stark contrast to make for the people. Just as the real Decapolis city blatantly shone forth Roman ideals, so too should you be a witness for God's ideals. Let your light (and lifestyle!) shine in such a way to bring God glory. Now that communicates well!

Also on the horizon line was the city of Tiberius, which was still under construction when Jesus was alive. Tiberius was one of Herod Antipas's projects. He governed the Jewish region of Galilee, and he envied all the benefits Rome could give. Like his father, Herod the Great, he used building projects as a display of his ego. However, the project at Tiberius was poorly planned and the expenses kept escalating. There were periodic pauses in construction while funds were acquired, leaving some buildings half built.[3] I can only imagine how amused the crowds were when Jesus talked about the cost of true discipleship and inserted,

> "Suppose one of you wants to build a tower. Won't you first sit down and estimate the cost to see if you have enough money to complete it? For if you lay the foundation and are not able to finish it, everyone who sees it will ridicule you, saying, 'This person began to build and wasn't able to finish.'" (Luke 14:28–30)

Although Jesus did not need to refer specifically to Antipas's folly, the crowd knew about these problematic building projects in Tiberius and to whom Jesus referred.

Jesus continued with another poke at Herod Antipas. Years before, Antipas visited Rome and fell in love with his half-brother's wife, Herodias. She agreed to marry him on condition that he divorce his current wife, Phasaelis, the daughter of Aretas, king of the Nabateans. The whole sordid affair was condemned by John the Baptist, which ultimately led to John's execution (Matt. 14:1–12; Mark 6:17–29; Luke 3:19–20). Phasaelis heard of the agreement between Antipas and Herodias and fled to her father's kingdom to inform Aretas of the shameful betrayal. The incident added a personal grievance to a long list of previous disputes Aretas had with Antipas, and the irate father immediately declared war on Antipas. When the two armies met for battle, the Nabatean king demolished Herod Antipas's army. As a follow-up to the political joke surrounding Antipas's building fiascos, Jesus said, "Or suppose a king is about to go to war against another king. Won't he first sit down and consider whether he is able with ten thousand men to oppose the one coming against him with twenty thousand?" (Luke 14:31). Not only would Jesus' Galilean audience have found humor in these examples, but his message was also clear: Do not be as foolish as Herod Antipas; the cost of discipleship was high and not to be considered lightly.

Parables

Jesus also wove together multilayered stories to engage people in the crowd and invite them into the process of learning. The parables Jesus told, which were deeply rooted in the Hebrew Scriptures, were meant to be discussed in community. Different layers of the parable emerged depending on if the listener recognized the hidden messages or references in the story. In modern vernacular, these are hidden references in video games or television shows and movies that are called "Easter eggs." They are semi-hidden references to something else that you can easily miss unless you are looking for them. Consider the movie *Shrek* that was released in 2001. It is a humorous movie all on its own, but if you recognize the references to *Crouching Tiger, Hidden Dragon* from 2000, or *The Matrix* from 1999, or to the wildly popular *Riverdance* from 1994, or *Robin Hood, Men in Tights* from 1993, then *Shrek* becomes even more hilarious.

Certainly, Jesus' parables can be read on their own, but they become deeply meaningful and sometimes more puzzling the more you understand the hidden references. This chapter is not the right place to explore all that the parables have to offer, but I do recommend a few resources at the end of this chapter to help you uncover more "Easter eggs" in the text.

Let us consider one famous parable that is typically called the "Prodigal Son." Jesus told the parable in response to the Pharisees and scribes who were grumbling that Jesus was eating with sinners. Remember that the Pharisees were deeply concerned with purity laws and with community. Since they wanted to usher society toward a stricter adherence to God's teachings, they thought that any self-respecting rabbi should not be sharing food with people generally considered as outcasts or sinners. Jesus responded with three stories about someone who lost something precious, spent valuable time to find it, and then elaborately celebrated the rediscovery (Luke 15). This theme is not uncommon from other stories of God searching and rejoicing over his lost people.

The third version of the parable added intrigue to the overall meaning behind Jesus' response: "There was a man with two sons . . . " Ah, the Pharisees had a framework for this kind of story. The Hebrew Bible has many stories with two brothers—Cain and Abel, Jacob and Esau, and so on. In these stories, the younger brother often usurps the older. But where did Jesus go with this particular story? The youngest son walked away from the family and became estranged from his father. This might have been another recognized pattern. Israel was God's son, and they walked away from their father who never gave up pursuing them. Several rabbis told similar stories to the one Jesus told, but those stories normally included only one son. Jesus' story had two. And Jesus inserted a plot twist, so the story did not unfold the way the listener would have anticipated. In several rabbinic parables, the father sent out an emissary (prophets) to plead with the son to return. In Jesus' parable, there were no emissaries. He left out that part.

If you were listening to Jesus' parable, you might have thought you were tracking with him and understanding his allusions to Israelite history. But you would have been puzzled by its ending. The younger son returned home to much rejoicing. Well, that part was expected. But the older son remained out in the field, seemingly ignorant of the feast happening in the house. The father went out to talk with his son, but then Jesus concluded with a cliff hanger. In the parable, there is no resolution of the tension. What happened to the older son? And for the listeners of the story, they were left with questions such as, "What is Jesus communicating with this parable?" and "Which character are we in this parable?" Were the scribes and Pharisees the rebellious younger son? Or maybe the older son? Did one of the characters in the parable represent the sinners with whom Jesus was eating? And which role did Jesus think he played? Was he the one in each of the three parables to seek that which was lost? That would be daring, because the father role (found in the third story) usually represented God. The answers to these questions were like puzzle pieces the listeners gathered to fit together the hidden message. Jesus did not always answer problematic questions with straightforward statements. He did not make the parables easy to understand, which forced the listeners to engage. Even two thousand years later, Jesus' parables evoke curiosity, and we continue to arrive at new answers for what each parable meant.[4]

Popular Fables

Along with references to modern political events and allusions to narratives in the Hebrew Bible, Jesus borrowed from a famous collection of fables attributed to Aesop.[5] These fables were in circulation for hundreds of years prior to Jesus and were well known and referenced in antiquity, including the Jewish community.

One fable that Jesus referenced was the fisherman and his flute. In this fable, the fisherman played his flute for the fish but the fish did not respond. So, the fisherman caught fish in a net and as they floundered outside the water, the fisherman said, "I say, enough of your dancing, since you refused to dance when I played my pipe for you before!" The fable was a cautionary tale of responding only when in dire circumstance and when the response was too late.

Skilled rabbis did not simply regurgitate these fables, but they reinterpreted the fables to fit their teachings.[6] So Jesus referenced this fable, albeit changing the fish to children. He spoke to the crowds about John the Baptist, who fascinated them and yet they ignored his warnings. Jesus quoted Malachi 3:1, "I will send my messenger, who will prepare the way before me." And here Jesus hints toward the Elijah-like role that John played (we talked about this in the last chapter). Some people in the crowds were baptized by John, but to those who were not, Jesus set up this comparison:

Jesus went on to say, "To what, then, can I compare the people of this generation? What are they like? They are like children sitting in the marketplace and calling out to each other:

"'We played the pipe for you,
>   and you did not dance;
> we sang a dirge,
>   and you did not cry.'" (Luke 7:31–32)

When interpreted with the reference to Malachi and the accepted meaning of the fable, Jesus' warning was clear. For those who refused to listen and heed the warnings (i.e., of John the Baptist), there would come a time when a response would be too late.

While in his home synagogue in Nazareth, Jesus shared a simple line from a fable about a fox and a frog. The fable tells of a frog claimed to cure all ailments with his physician's skill, but the clever fox exposed the frog's lies by challenging the frog: "How can you claim to cure the sickness of others when there are signs of sickness on your face?" In the Nazareth synagogue, Jesus read from the book of Isaiah that the time of redemption was near. The people were excited about his teaching, until he turned the tables on them. "Surely you will quote this proverb to me: 'Physician, heal yourself!' And you will tell me, 'Do here in your hometown what we have heard that you did in Capernaum'" (Luke 4:23). In this case, the words of the fable put into the mouths of the people in the synagogue pointed toward the villagers' doubt that Jesus' words were true. Jesus went on to say that the promises from Isaiah were indeed taking place, but the people of Nazareth would miss it. Not surprisingly, the audience was offended by Jesus' rebuke, and as one group, they rushed to push him off of a cliff.

Let us consider one more fable: the wolf in sheep's clothing. The wolf had trouble catching a sheep to eat because of the shepherds' attentiveness. The wolf solved his problem by clothing himself in a discarded sheepskin and joining the flock. Almost immediately, the wolf managed to snag a sheep for lunch. That evening, however, one of the shepherds decided that he was in the mood for mutton broth. He grabbed the first sheep he found, which happened to be the wolf. The wolf was used for soup.

Jesus' skill at layering meanings in a single phrase is evident in how he used this fable. In Israelite literature, wolves were commonly used to describe the unfaithful leaders who destroyed God's flock (Zeph. 3:3). Ezekiel says the leaders "are like wolves tearing their prey; they shed blood and kill people to make unjust gain" (Ezek. 22:27). So, there is a possible correlation between the unfaithful leaders and Aesop's tale of the wolf who devours the sheep. Although the Israelite narratives do not portray a wolf in sheep's clothing, Jesus made the connection. "Watch out for false prophets. They come to you in sheep's clothing, but inwardly they are ferocious wolves" (Matt. 7:15). In other words, be wary of those who hide their true nature. Jesus did not mention unfaithful leaders, but some in the crowd may have understood the connection. Jesus continued to teach that a person's true character was determined by the fruit of their actions.

Teaching with Authority

As people listened to Jesus' skilled teachings, they began to attribute to him the honorific title of "Rabbi." He certainly seemed to fulfill that role. Rabbis were skilled interpreters of written and oral law, and they taught with actions as well as words. Rabbis had disciples who soaked in their teacher's behaviors, teachings, and habits of rest and study. Jesus did all of these things.

Some of the Jewish leaders, observing Jesus' unorthodox behavior and the crowd's willingness to call him rabbi, questioned his authority. Jesus did not have the same recognized pattern of training to which they were accustomed, and yet he carried on sustained theological conversations with them about Scripture and oral traditions. With which master-teacher had Jesus studied to speak authoritatively about a proper interpretation of the Torah? Who gave him the authority to fulfill the position of a rabbi?

When interrogated on such matters, Jesus drew a correlation between himself and one of Israel's greatest prophets, Moses. The book of Exodus says that Moses ascended Mount Sinai to receive the Torah from God. A commonly accepted teaching from the Jewish sages said that Moses *explained* the Torah to Joshua, Joshua taught it to the elders, the elders taught it to the prophets, and finally the prophets to the people (Avot 1:1). This teaching referred to receiving both instruction and authority. Moses was the only one not granted authority from a human teacher; he received his from God. If the teachers believed that Moses had authority, then why not Jesus who claimed similar God-given authority? (Matt. 21:23, Mark 11:27–28; Luke 20:1–2).

The book of Deuteronomy promises that God will raise up another prophet like Moses and put his words in the prophet's mouth (Deut. 18:15–18). In the context of Deuteronomy, it is unclear whether such a prophet was a singular prophet or one in a successive line of prophets like Moses. In the Gospel of Matthew, we see references to Jesus' Moses-like authority. For the setting of the Sermon on the Mount, Matthew said Jesus went *up a mountain* and *taught the Torah* to the people, similar to Moses. Jesus got to the heart of what the law was intended to do. He did not abolish but fulfilled the Torah through his own actions (Matt. 5:17). Jesus called the people back to the law and to what covenant faithfulness was really all about: loving God with your whole heart, soul, and strength (cf. Deut. 6:5). Matthew's description places Jesus even closer to Deuteronomy's "prophet like Moses." Potentially others in Jesus' day made a similar connection, because when considering who Jesus was, some suggested he was "*the* Prophet," a possible reference back to Deuteronomy (John 1:21, 25).

Some of Jesus' contemporaries, however, did not see Jesus fitting the Moses pattern but rather that of the promised Elijah figure from the book of Malachi (Matt. 16:14; Mark 6:15; 8:28; Luke 9:19). In the last chapter, we talked about this pattern and how it underscored the significance of Jesus' baptism. Written after the death and resurrection of Jesus, the Gospels associate John the Baptist with the Elijah figure in Malachi. But some people, who listened to Jesus teach and did not have hindsight working in their favor, concluded that Jesus could have been the Elijah figure instead of John.

Jesus certainly embodied aspects of the Israelite prophets who critiqued their own culture from within and who opposed the status quo. They were called to encourage the people to remain faithful to their covenant with God and to invest in a society that reflected a God-designed kingdom. The prophets often asked the Israelites to turn away from their current lifestyle and instead choose to accept what God desired. A major role for the prophets was teaching the Israelites how to interpret the Torah for their time period. In other words, the prophetic message was an invitation to belong to God's kingdom and to *act* like a resident of the kingdom. Jesus' message was similar. He did not tell the Jews to abandon the Torah or the God of their ancestors. When Jesus taught and healed people, he claimed both the manifestation of the kingdom of God in the here and now (Luke 11:20; 17:21) and also God's sovereignty over human affairs.[7]

To demonstrate the totality of the restoration God desired in his kingdom, Jesus performed miracles such as healing and even bringing the dead back to life. Salvation was God's liberating power that broke the bonds of oppression and set people free. Keep in mind that Jesus was teaching a community-minded people. First-century Jews did not have the same individualistic mind-set that Westerners have today. The Jewish people understood themselves as existing in an ancient and continuing story that included both their ancestors and their descendants. Although anticipating a singular Messiah, the whole community would be redeemed and brought into God's kingdom. Jesus lived the kingdom message, and the kind of kingdom Jesus spoke of was not a kingdom applicable only to the rich or the religious. No matter their gender, age, socioeconomic status, or political leanings, Jesus invited them all into the conversation about God's kingdom.

Conclusion

The crowds that followed Jesus were compiled of fishermen, traders, farmers, crafters, skilled educators, and members of the Jewish elite. The majority of the crowd depended on subsistence living and thus lived close to nature. Life was demanding, and for these people, spirituality had to be applicable in this world.[8] For some modern Christians, religion is discussed as a bodiless spiritual reality detached from this world. But that concept is an idea influenced by the Greek idea of a *psyche* (soul or spirit) that was considered to be the immortal part of a person.[9] Jews, however, talked about a *lived* theology that influenced people's lives in their immediate context. Jesus taught within this environment in which God's redemption was thought of as pertaining to the collective whole, not the individual soul. Salvation was for the community, and the kingdom for a group of people.

Throughout Jesus' public ministry, he interacted with a large variety of people with diverse experiences, depending on their family trade and where they lived. Within the crowds were men, women, children, Jews and Gentiles, Roman citizens, and soldiers. There were Hellenistic-loving Jews, conservative isolationists, and fiery Zealots, and Jesus interacted with all of them. He was a master communicator who used technical speech, parables, examples from the land, and popular fables to resonate with the cultural reality of each audience. He spoke with the political elite in Jerusalem, those well educated in the law, and those who were hard-working commoners. To all of his listeners, though, Jesus taught about the restoration God sought to bring to his people, and he invited them to catch the vision of the kingdom of God grounded in the here and now on earth as in heaven.

9

Passion Week

Although Jesus and his disciples regularly walked to Jerusalem for important Jewish festivals, no other journey was as significant as this final one. The Gospel of Luke describes how they slowly made their way to Jerusalem—through Galilee, down the Jordan River Valley, across the river near Jericho, and up into the Judean hills to Jerusalem. The group was making the journey to celebrate the Passover. All the teachings, miracles, and debates in Jesus' public ministry led to this final week in Jerusalem. With the simple act of riding into the city on a donkey, Jesus ushered in a dramatic and unexpected conclusion to his earthly ministry.

Entering Jerusalem

Political, social, and religious significance penetrated every event in Jesus' final week in Jerusalem. If you revisit the agricultural calendar discussed in chapter 2, you will remember that Passover occurred at the beginning of the barley harvest. The population numbers in Jerusalem swelled as Jews from the diaspora traveled to Jerusalem to celebrate the Passover. The city could not house everyone, so many pilgrims either lived in temporary structures on the western slope of the Mount of Olives or stayed with friends in the surrounding area. Jesus and his disciples likely stayed in Bethany with their good friends, Mary, Martha, and Lazarus.

For anyone who supported Rome, this holiday was a tense week. Passover evoked memories for the Jews of a time when God triumphed over Pharaoh and redeemed his people out of slavery in Egypt. The city was packed with visitors celebrating the overthrow of a foreign power, which only heightened the population's anti-Roman sentiments. As previous Passover festivals had been the context for riots, everyone would have to be on guard.

Throughout Jesus' ministry, he taught his disciples the truth of God's kingdom. Yet even those who lived with him, watched him perform miracles, and walked in his dust expected this kingdom to be an earthly kingdom in the fashion of King David's. So, although Jesus did not intend to inaugurate a Jewish kingdom in Jerusalem, that was exactly what people wanted from him. Therefore, the political tension in the city, along with the expectations of the people of what Jesus would do, laid the groundwork for an unexpected and dramatic conclusion to this week.

On the first day of that memorable week, Jesus requested a donkey on which to ride the short descent down the Mount of Olives and into the city (Matt. 21:1–3; Mark 11:1–3; Luke 19:29–31; John 12:12–16). This may seem like an odd request. Certainly, he was not too tired to walk. Even though the donkey was a common beast of burden, riding on one made a striking political assertion about Jesus' authority in the city. Horses were war animals, and an authoritative figure riding into a city on one was akin to declaring war on the city. In contrast, a political figure who rode a donkey was a sign of peace and demonstrated that the ruler already had control over the city (cf. 1 Kings 1:32–35). So, Jesus entered Jerusalem with the confidence of a political ruling figure, who already had authority over the city. The Gospel writers associated Jesus' actions with the writings of the post-exilic prophet, Zechariah, who preached a message of hope for God's restoration. The second half of this book speaks of a God who is jealous for Zion and who returns to dwell in a glorified city. When enemy nations are destroyed, Israel's king arrives "humble, and mounted on a donkey" (Zech. 9:9). Zechariah was not *predicting* Jesus, but the Gospel writers made the connection that Jesus, as the promised king, was fulfilling God's promised redemption.

Jesus' arrival caused a stir, and a multitude of people went out to usher him into the city. Consider the diversity in the crowds following Jesus, and recall that many in the crowd were pilgrims coming from other locations. Think, too, about how geography affects people's openness to new ideas, and that these events took place in the Judean hills. In the crowd on that particular day, we can assume there were those who only heard rumors of Jesus, those who interacted with him in Galilee, and those who held to the more conservative views common in Jerusalem.

Even with such diversity in the crowd, the majority of people were filled with hope and expectation about who Jesus was. With a little imagination, you can listen to the buzz of the crowds, feel the energy of people as they focused their attention on this one man, and hear the swell of music as people began to sing hymns of liberation and shout for God to restore freedom to his people. Matthew (21:9) and John (12:13) state that the crowds accompanied him shouting *Hosanna!* ("God save us!") and singing,

> Give thanks to the LORD, for he is good;
> > his love endures forever. (Ps. 118:1)

What festive lyrics to sing as the crowd entered Jerusalem!

> LORD, save us!
> > LORD, grant us success!
> Blessed is he who comes in the name of the LORD. (Ps. 118:25–26)

The hope that God would once again deliver Israel throbbed through the crowd. The atmosphere was thick with cries for God to save his people in this day, as he had against the Egyptians and against the Seleucids.

Just as significant was the nervous dread of the Jewish leaders in Jerusalem. They understood the complex religious and political web of relationships they had with the Roman officials, and they feared the crowd's enthusiasm. This is reflected in the plea of the Pharisees during Jesus' entrance to the city to "rebuke your disciples!" (Luke 19:39). Perhaps some of the Jewish elite in Jerusalem expected Rome to kill this leader, as they had killed previous messianic figures, or perhaps they thought the people themselves were in danger of Roman retaliation against this public demonstration of resistance.[1]

Notice the juxtaposition between the hope and joy of the people and the sadness of Jesus when he saw the city and wept over it (Luke 19:41). A story of great magnitude was unfolding, but Jesus alone understood the big picture. Pilgrims walking over the Mount of Olives had a sweeping view of the temple and the rest of the city around it. Even in the midst of a grand celebratory entrance to Jerusalem, with his eyes on the city, Jesus lamented the tragedy that would occur only forty years later when the Romans destroyed the temple and slaughtered residents of the city (Luke 19:42–44).

Now, shift perspective to the Roman guards stationed at the Antonia Fortress that was perched on the northwest corner of the temple mount platform. Perhaps from their vantage point, they watched the crowds joyfully enter the city, singing songs of liberation and waving palm branches. They would have noticed the political acts of resistance. Everything about the situation screamed danger and emphasized the possibility of a bloody revolt. The soldiers would have to be on high alert all week.

Jesus entered as one who had a right to the city. Luke 19:45 says that Jesus went directly to the temple where he found the business of buying and selling, which belonged on the streets of Jerusalem, occurring within sacred space (Matt. 21:12; Mark 11:11; Luke 19:45–47). He drove out the merchants and quoted the words of Jeremiah: "Has this house, which bears my Name, become a den of robbers to you?" (Jer. 7:11). Jeremiah's words were a part of the prophet's scathing rebuke against the temple authorities, whom he says were responsible for the temple's destruction.[2] Jesus used Jeremiah's words to rebuke the priests who should have maintained the sanctity of the temple, while simultaneously claiming himself to be the one legitimately in charge of God's house.

The events of this single day were dramatic and set the tone for the week to come. Jesus majestically entered a Roman-controlled Jerusalem with people singing songs and waving palm branches. He then cleansed the temple. The picture is reminiscent of one hundred years prior, when Judas Maccabaeus led a ragtag group of resistors against the Seleucids and freed Jerusalem from their rule. They too celebrated the liberation of the city by singing songs, waving palm branches, and cleansing the temple. Now in the same city, a different international power was in charge. The crowd that ushered Jesus into Jerusalem celebrated the arrival of the one they thought would liberate them from the Romans. These were dramatic and dangerous actions in front of the Roman soldiers and in front of any Jewish leader invested in maintaining Roman control of Jerusalem!

A Week in Jerusalem

As we have seen so far, Jerusalem was a joyful, bustling city during the Passover festival but with underlying tensions. Jesus made a grand entrance to the city and cleansed the temple—both dramatic actions—but what proper authority did Jesus have to do either? Throughout this week, the chief priest and elders would approach Jesus to probe this issue of his authority.

As Jesus taught in the temple complex, the people flocked to hear his words. Among them were religious leaders testing Jesus on complicated matters of the law. The Herodians (who were pro-Rome) asked questions about the legality of paying taxes to Caesar. The Sadducees (who did not believe in resurrection) asked Jesus to solve a riddle involving marriage, resurrection, and the Mosaic Law. An expert in the law asked Jesus to name the most significant law in the Torah. All of the thorny questions about the intricacy of the Torah and the role of the Roman government were designed to uncover Jesus' agenda and to create a definitive reason to kill him. But Jesus had perfect answers every time for their complicated questions. The leaders may have wanted to silence Jesus, but the crowd protected him and frustrated the leaders' plans.

Every day Jesus taught in the temple, but at night he went outside the city walls to spend the night on the Mount of Olives. When the time came to celebrate the Passover meal, Jesus asked Peter and John to make the proper arrangements in a house within the city walls (Matt. 26:17–29; Mark 14:12–25; Luke 22:7–20). That evening, Jesus and his disciples gathered to share a festive meal that commemorated the exodus from Egypt. Although the specifics of the menu are not listed in the Gospels, the table would have been filled with wine, lamb, bitter herbs, unleavened bread, and possibly dried fruit for dessert. During the course of the meal, Jesus took the meanings behind the significant elements of the memorial feast and attached them to himself. The unleavened bread was his body, and the wine was his blood. These were symbols of the new covenant, a new exodus, and a new redemption.[3] For those participating in the meal, Jesus' words were obscure, and they may have asked themselves how any of this was possible.

At the conclusion of the long meal—which was celebratory but perhaps also a bit somber and confusing—the small group left the house and walked out into the night. Meanwhile, Judas left the feast to inform the chief priest of the opportunity to arrest Jesus that night. The chief priest could not arrest Jesus within the city walls, where a commotion within the densely populated city would draw too much attention, but the plan to arrest Jesus in the darkness of night outside the perimeter of the city was ideal. The chief priest and Jewish authorities gathered their police force, and due to Jesus' popularity and the likelihood of revolt, Roman soldiers accompanied them.

Given the late hour and the location outside the city walls, the significance of the events that night was not immediately obvious to those with him, encamped on the hill.

As Jesus and the disciples walked to the Mount of Olives—as was his custom at the end of the day (Luke 21:37; 22:39)—he stopped at a quiet place and invited his disciples to pray. The Gospel of Luke says Jesus was in agony and prayed fervently (22:44). In this moment, Jesus had to make a choice. He could continue along the road, and in only a few moments be over the Mount of Olives where he could disappear into the wilderness and avoid the impending hours of torture. Or Jesus could stay where he was and wait for the soldiers to arrest him. The anguish of the moment is evident in his prayer: "Father, if you are willing, take this cup from me; yet not my will, but yours be done" (Luke 22:42; cf. Matt. 26:39; Mark 14:36). In other words, if there is a Plan B, God, this is a good time to make it known! But if not, he would honor God over his own choices.

John's Gospel is unique in how it communicates the significance of Jesus' choice to choose to follow God's plan. The whole design of the Gospel depicts a new creation story. The first words in John, "In the beginning," remind the reader of Genesis—the goodness of God's creation and the brokenness that came from humanity's choices in Eden. Of all the Gospel writers, John is the only one to say that Jesus and the disciples stopped to pray in a *garden* (18:1). The new-creation theme in John should make us consider the humans in the garden of Eden. Like them, Jesus had a choice to make in another garden. Only one option provided the solution to the brokenness of all of creation. Only one choice could lead to the restored relationship between God and humans and creation. In the garden of Gethsemane, Jesus made the difficult choice to follow God's version of good over his own self-preservation.

The Trial

The soldiers arrested Jesus and took him to the high priest's home (Matt. 26:47–57; Mark 14:43–54; Luke 22:47–54; John 18:3–13). Although the exact location of the home is not known, archaeological excavations provide helpful clues. Close to Herod's palace (at this time occupied by Pilate) was a neighborhood with huge, ornate, expensive homes designed around an open-aired courtyard with walls and gates blocking the view from the street. Archaeologists have found a large number of expensive stone vessels (used for purity reasons) and ritual purity baths among the ruins, which suggests that the homes belonged to the wealthy priestly class.[4] Although it is impossible to know which house belonged to the high priest, the house was certainly in that neighborhood.

The Gospels mention Jesus' imprisonment overnight at Caiaphas's house, and they mention Jesus' trial before the Sanhedrin. But the exact timing of all the details is uncertain. Was the trial at night and in secret as John implies (John 18:28)? Were there subsequent trial-related events in the morning as Matthew, Mark, and Luke suggest (Matt. 27:1–2; Mark 15:1; Luke 22:66)? While accounts are varied, details suggest that there was a secretive pretrial at Caiaphas's house and a semiformal trial before the Sanhedrin during the day. No matter how much he wanted to, Caiaphas alone could not issue a death warrant; he needed the Sanhedrin's cooperation.[5] Although the high priest did not like Jesus, he still had to establish his guilt according to Jewish law before seeking Roman punishment.

The Sanhedrin, who functioned as the supreme Jewish court and acted according to the standards of Jewish law, had the authority to convict Jesus but only with concurring testimony by two witnesses. Mark 14:56 states that although many testified, the statements did not agree. The most inflammatory reports were the ones that recalled Jesus saying, "I will destroy this temple made with human hands and in three days will build another, not made with hands"—a claim that carried royal connotations.[6] To understand why everyone was upset, consider the rich history connecting Israelite kings to the Jerusalem temple—the conception and building of the first temple by David and Solomon, the cleansing of the temple by Hezekiah and Josiah, and the rebuilding and cleansing of the temple by Zerubbabel and Joshua. Then Judas Maccabaeus cleansed the temple and reinstituted a priestly dynasty. Even Herod the Great tried to claim a legitimate dynasty by rebuilding the temple. And now Jesus made similar claims. The leaders possibly heard echoes of Zechariah 6:12, which states that when God restored his people, the "Branch" (or messianic figure) would build the Lord's temple. When Jesus said that he would rebuild the temple, we usually interpret this as referring to his body in his resurrection, but the leaders interpreted him as assuming religious and royal authority.

Jesus' claim about the temple, therefore, provoked indignation and prompted the high priest to ask him, "Are you the Christ?" This is not a question about Jesus belonging to the Trinity or being the incarnation of God. It is a question of Jesus' claim to be the Messiah. In other words, did Jesus claim political and religious leadership over the Jewish people? Jesus responded in the affirmative and added, "But from now on the Son of Man will be seated at the right hand of God," which is a quote from Psalm 110. Although David wrote this psalm, in it the one he calls "my Lord" is summoned to sit at God's right hand. The context suggests that the enthroned figure is the Messiah, whose enemies are placed under his feet.[7] Additionally, Matthew and Mark add that Jesus concluded his Psalm 110 reference with the phrase "coming on the clouds of heaven," which is a reference from Daniel 7. The entirety of Daniel 7 speaks of the coming messianic figure who brings judgment against Israel's enemies, the end of the people's suffering, and the establishment of an everlasting kingdom. When Jesus uses Psalm 110 and Daniel 7 while speaking to the chief priest, he is affirming his role as Messiah and claiming that he will sit in judgment over all who oppose him. In that moment, those opposing him happened to be the chief priest and the Sanhedrin. Jesus' simple phrase not only claims God-given authority, but it also turns the tables against those judging him. This was a bold claim and an insult against the high priest. It is not surprising, then, that after this interaction the Jewish leaders demanded Jesus' execution.

The high priest's strategy was to show that Jesus was a political threat against Rome. As the governor of Judea, Pilate upheld Caesar's interests, collected taxes, and kept the peace. Roman authorities intervened in all matters involving violations of public order or movements of revolt, and they were allowed to revoke the Sanhedrin's jurisdiction or reverse their judgments. In this case, however, standing in agreement with the religious leaders to suppress messianic ideas was in Pilate's best interests.

Even before Jesus' trial, Pilate had a confrontational reputation.[8] He was abusive, cruel, and known to execute prisoners without trials. Pilate was not only devoted to the Roman emperor, but he also had a long history of conflict with the Jews. Years before Jesus' trial, Pilate had tried to install gold-plated shields in the palace in Jerusalem. Even though the shields did not contain images, they claimed Caesar was the son of the divine Augustus.

The Jews were understandably upset, yet Pilate's vindictiveness prevented him from taking down the shields. Only in response to a direct order from Caesar did Pilate remove them from Jerusalem and install them instead in Caesarea.

When the Jewish leaders brought Jesus before Pilate claiming that Jesus was a political adversary of Rome, Pilate was caught between his desire to snub his subjects and his fear of being labeled an enemy to Caesar.[9] He therefore tried to skirt responsibility. Since Herod Antipas, the ruler of Galilee, was in Jerusalem for the Passover, Pilate sent Jesus off to see him. After all, Jesus spent most of his time in Galilee. Antipas questioned Jesus at some length, but since Jesus remained silent, Antipas sent him back to Pilate (Luke 23:6–11).

One more option remained for Pilate. In prison awaiting execution was the Jewish extremist, Barabbas. There is actually no historical evidence outside of the Gospels that Rome was in the habit of releasing a prisoner during Passover. After all, such a tradition gained nothing for Rome. Rome was intolerant of adversaries, and Barabbas was an insurrectionist. He was also a local hero and executing him during the Passover holiday practically guaranteed unrest. Hypothetically, keeping Barabbas alive could potentially prevent citywide riots. In contrast, Jesus was not the ordinary sort of revolutionary, and it is unlikely that Pilate thought he was dangerous; but releasing a prisoner gave Pilate an advantage. Someone would die for rebelling against Rome. Would it be Barabbas or Jesus? If the Jewish leaders chose, then Pilate could shrug his shoulders and absolve himself of any consequences. Pilate washed his hands and pretended to be innocent for something that lay completely within his power to prevent. A riot was less likely to happen if the Jewish leaders who gathered at his palace chose which man would die. So, Pilate asked the question and hesitated long enough for the crowd to demand the death of Jesus.

Pilate turned Jesus over to the Roman soldiers, who scorned and ridiculed Jesus. Inside the Roman Praetorium, they tormented Jesus by placing a thorny crown on his head, putting a royal robe on him, and a staff in his right hand. Then they knelt down and said, "Hail, king of the Jews!" (Matt. 27:29). Their actions were not only a mockery of Jesus but also of the whole Jewish hope of freedom. Then Jesus was escorted out to die a publicly humiliating death on a cross like a common criminal.

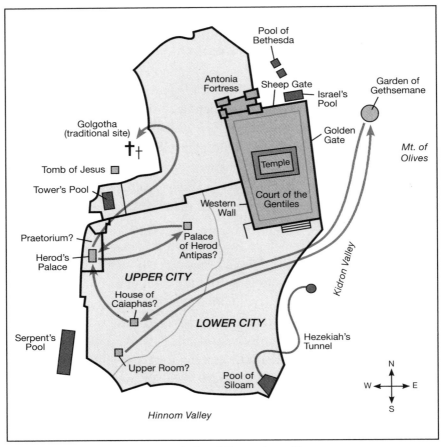

Figure 21. Trial and Execution of Jesus.

At this point, we must pause to think about the context of these complicated events. Maybe you have heard it said that the crowd that ushered Jesus into the city is the same crowd that called out for his death. By paying attention to the events around the trial, and to where in the city these things happened, that statement is not a fair conclusion. Jesus was arrested in the middle of the night. The events at Caiaphas's house did not happen according to Jewish law and could therefore be considered illegal. The high priest's home was close to the palaces of Pilate and Herod Antipas. The trial basically happened behind closed doors, so there was no way the thousands of pilgrims in the city knew what was happening. The people who put so much hope in Jesus, and who ushered him into the city with singing and celebration, suddenly found their Messiah horrifically crucified as a public display of what happens to all who confront Rome.

Death and Victory

The Roman soldiers crucified Jesus on an exposed hill outside the city's walls, along with two criminals. A sign with the words THIS IS JESUS, THE KING OF THE JEWS was placed over his head in mockery of his failed mission against Rome. For hours, Jesus hung on the cross and endured the insults hurled at him by soldiers, passersby, and even the criminals crucified with him.

The Gospel writers chose to emphasize different details from Jesus' last moments. Luke and John describe his compassion by his forgiveness of the one criminal and his unfaltering concern for his mother before he "gave up his spirit." Matthew and Mark chose to report that prior to taking his last breath, Jesus quoted the first line of Psalm 22, "My God, my God, why have you forsaken me?" Although these words make it seem that Jesus was claiming that God had deserted him, he was actually referring to the lesson of the whole psalm. When read in its entirety, this psalm begins with the author crying out in desolation but then proclaiming trust in God's everlasting power, and finally declaring the everlasting victory of God over evil.

> All the ends of the earth
>   will remember and turn to the LORD,
> and all the families of the nations
>   will bow down before him,
> for dominion belongs to the LORD
>   and he rules over the nations. . . .
> They will proclaim his righteousness,
>   declaring to a people yet unborn:
> He has done it! (Ps. 22:27–28, 31)

Far from accusing God of turning his face away, Jesus' final words were a powerful declaration that although his present circumstances were dire, God's kingdom was victoriously established in that moment.

Conclusion

Jesus' final week in Jerusalem began with a celebratory procession into the city and concluded with a shameful execution outside the city walls. No one fully understood the significance of what Jesus chose to do. For the crowds of people, Jesus' execution was the death of their hope for redemption. In reality, his execution was the victory of God over sin and death and the beginning of a new narrative of restoration.

10

From Death to New Life

When the Gospel writers describe the horrific details of Jesus' crucifixion, they also give subtle words of reassurance to their readers that death may not be the end of his mission. In telling the story of Jesus resurrecting Lazarus, John foreshadows Jesus' power over death (John 11:38–44). Matthew documents the proclamation of Jesus' innocence by Pilate's wife (Matt. 27:19). Luke records belief in Jesus from the thief on the cross, and also the soldier's recognition of Jesus' righteousness (Luke 23:40–43, 47). John demonstrates the deep compassion Jesus exhibited in the final moments of his life (John 19:26–27), while Matthew and Mark describe Jesus' death with the words of Psalm 22 on his lips. Each of these declarations hint that the story is not yet over, because death was not the end. The climax of the narrative comes with the victory of life over death.

Later readers of the Gospels can anticipate the resurrection, but for those who lived the events in real time, Jesus' crucifixion was traumatic. The man to whom the disciples dedicated years of their lives, and the man whose every movement and teachings they absorbed—that man was dead. The rabbi they followed, who promised that God's kingdom had arrived and was accessible to all people, was killed by the empire they had hoped their teacher would overthrow. Rome appeared victorious, and the followers of Jesus were vulnerable to possible retaliation.

At this point in the narrative, Western Protestants tend to rush from the horror of the crucifixion on Friday to the joy of resurrection on Sunday. I can understand the urge, but there is value in recognizing the difficulty of the Saturday wait. I remember living in Jerusalem and participating in the Orthodox Church's remembrance of the last week of Jesus' life. I found deep meaning in intentionally and patiently moving from place to place to remember the details of the week, but I felt like I was moving in slow motion, which made me feel impatient. That is when I realized what little patience I have with the suffering aspect of this narrative. I am familiar with darkness and despair. Life has taught me that. I was anxious to get to joy. Reliving the Passion story in real time and within the historic place where the events happened was deeply sobering. But I learned that to fully understand Resurrection Sunday, I could not hurry through the pain of the days before it.

Now I try to slow down and consider what the crowds and Jesus' disciples were thinking and feeling after Jesus was laid in the tomb and the stone rolled into place. It is quite possible that those who cheered for Jesus as he entered Jerusalem at the beginning of the week experienced a wide variety of emotions. Maybe they were disappointed that Jesus did not seem to be who they hoped he would be, or maybe they experienced a high level of uncertainty about the ramifications of publicly supporting the man killed by those in power. I wonder if those who gathered on Saturday for fellowship and mutual support were overcome with deep sorrow and confusion of the wait. They experienced the death of their dreams and expectations. Did they doubt now why they had chosen to follow this man? Were they confused by all the times Jesus confirmed he was the Messiah? Did they begin to reconsider the statements Jesus made about needing to go to Jerusalem to die? The death of Jesus must have seemed like a death of hope. Their inspirational rabbi—the one in whom hundreds of people had put their hope—had been executed. Those in power continued to control the series of events during the Passover festival, and the status quo continued. For the disciples, this particular Passover week, which began with Jesus' majestic entrance into Jerusalem, ended on a heartbreaking note.

Then, on the first day of the new week, some of the women went to the tomb, only to rush back with a report that Jesus' body was not there. Angels had told them that Jesus had risen from the dead! Could the listeners legitimately dare to hope that the women's reports were true and that Jesus was alive again? A couple of disciples ran to check, and the tomb was definitely empty. This was an unexpected added element to the drama. I wonder how long it took for the disciples to remember the comments Jesus had previously made about being killed and raised to life again (Matt. 16:21; Mark 8:31–32; 14:28; Luke 9:20–21).

The Gospels of Matthew and Mark end rather abruptly after the resurrection. Luke and John, however, give their readers extended conversations between Jesus and his disciples after the resurrection. Let us look first at Luke's account before moving on to John's.

Post-Resurrection: Luke

In the afternoon of the day of resurrection, two disciples left Jerusalem and set off on the road down the steep western side of the hills to Emmaus (Luke 24:13–31).[1] The two were deep in conversation about Jesus' brutal death and the unexpected news of the resurrection. Jesus joined them on the road, although they did not recognize him and thought he was a stranger. As they ruminated over the week's drama, the stranger with them seemed unaware of the latest news, which further confused the disciples. How was it possible for someone *not* to know was going on? The two described the recent events to the newcomer, and their heartbreak is almost palpable in their comment, "We had hoped that he was the one who was going to redeem Israel" (v. 21). They then expressed additional confusion from that morning when the women reported that Jesus' body was missing from the tomb.

The stranger replied to the men, "How foolish you are, and how slow to believe all that the prophets have spoken!" (v. 25). Then Jesus continued with an explanation for which I wish I had been present! Using the books of Moses and the prophets, Jesus explained everything in Scripture that concerned himself.

Think back to chapter 1 where I highlighted narratives and patterns from the Old Testament. I wonder to which patterns and themes Jesus drew the disciples' attention, and how he reshaped their expectations about the messianic purpose. I imagine the disciples' minds sparking with new insights into Jesus' life in light of Jesus' explanation. Did Jesus start with the creation narratives and God's design to have a place in which humans freely came into his sacred presence, and how that communion was shattered? Death was the consequence of sin, but that death came in the form of exile from the perfect place of creation (Gen. 2:16; 3:22–24). Did Jesus rehearse the covenants God made with his people? Did he explain how the Torah was meant to restore the relationship between God and humans and nature? Did he highlight God's priority for his people to be a light to the world and to function as a world-*influencing* kingdom instead of a world-*dominating* kingdom? Given the prophetic pattern of repent, return, and restore, did Jesus fully explain what this restoration looked like? I certainly wish I knew!

What we do know is that Jesus used the Scriptures to make sense of his role in God's bigger narrative. The exile was over, but not because Jewish people returned to the land that formerly belonged to the Israelite kingdom. Restoration did not require a reestablished Israelite kingdom like King David's. Restoration came through conquering the death that was humanity's exile from the perfect place of creation. Through Jesus, the ultimate exile—separation from God—ended. God established his kingdom on earth, and his kingdom was not evident in human power and prestige, but in the changed lives of the citizens of the kingdom. While the Jews anticipated the restoration of a human kingdom, God's vision was bigger. He was restoring all of creation.

I imagine that for the two disciples on the road to Emmaus, the conversation shifted their perspective on Scripture and shed light on the significance of the past week's events. As evening approached, they asked the stranger to stay with them and share a meal. When Jesus broke the bread, the disciples finally realized who was with them—the resurrected Jesus. Jesus then immediately disappeared. The two disciples could not contain their excitement over the implications of their new understanding of Scripture, and they ran *up* to Jerusalem. That incline was no joke! But they could not be prevented from sharing their new insights with the others in Jerusalem.

Post-Resurrection: John

With echoes and resonances of the Genesis creation stories, the Gospel of John explains Jesus' role in the new creation narrative. John sets the intention of the book with the first words, "In the beginning." He continues with listing a series of "signs" to prove who Jesus was, with the seventh and final sign being the resurrection of Lazarus from the dead. In the previous chapter, I drew your attention to Jesus' courageous prayer in the garden of Gethsemane, with his declaration that he (unlike the first humans in the first garden) would follow God's will and not his own. Jesus was crucified on the sixth day of the week, and John records Jesus' final words as "It is finished" (19:30).

But the Gospel's narrative is not finished. If we follow John's pattern, the seventh day of creation was the day of rest. In Genesis, when God rests on the seventh day, the language suggests that God sat as the proper king enthroned over all creation. John's Gospel suggests that Jesus finished the work of re-creation on Friday and on Saturday he rested. Through Jesus, the power of death of exile was overturned and a new story of creation began.

As all of the Gospels record, on the first day of the week (Matt. 28:1; Mark 16:2; Luke 24:1; John 20:1), the women were the first to go to the tomb where Jesus was buried. But when John tells the story, he specifies that Mary went to see the empty tomb, and there in the *garden* she saw someone she assumed to be the *gardener*. The image here is beautiful. The resurrected Jesus was the gardener of a new creation. Jesus was a new Adam figure, and his victory over death was the first day of the new creation.

Unlike Matthew and Mark, the Gospel of John does not record specific instructions for Jesus' followers to meet him in Galilee (Matt. 28:7, 10; Mark 14:28; 16:7). John does, however, give his readers an extended narrative of a meeting between Jesus and his disciples along the shoreline of the Sea of Galilee. The disciples had gone to the place where they spent the most time with Jesus, but what should they do while waiting? The disciples did what they knew best: fishing. Fishermen worked during the night so fish could not see the thick cotton threads of the net in the water; but on this particular night, the disciples were not successful. As the morning light dawned, Jesus stood on the shoreline, but the disciples did not recognize him. He asked if they had caught any fish, and when they responded in the negative, he told them to cast their net on the right side of the boat.

I wonder if in this moment Peter experienced déjà vu regarding an event three years earlier. Luke tells of a night similar to this one when Peter had an unproductive night of fishing and was sitting on the shore in the morning light mending the nets. Jesus stepped into Peter's boat and pushed away from shore to make use of the water's amplification to teach to the gathering crowd. Upon concluding, Jesus told Peter to cast his net into the water. The instructions were impractical. Any good fisherman knew that fishing during the day, especially after all the shouting and commotion on the surface of the water, was unfeasible. What did a man from Nazareth know about fishing anyway? Why should a lifelong fisherman follow the instructions from a man who grew up in the hills? But Peter followed Jesus' instructions and ended up catching an exorbitant amount of fish (Luke 5:1–11).

Years later, after another frustrating night on the water, Peter heard those familiar words of encouragement: "Throw your net on the right side of the boat" (John 21:6). The disciples obeyed, and they caught so many fish that they could not pull up the nets. John was the first to identify the man on the shore as Jesus, but Peter's excitement was such that he immediately dove into the water to swim ashore.

When the disciples pulled the boat out of the water, they saw Jesus cooking fish over a coal fire, which is an interesting detail for John to include, especially given the way smells provoke memories. The last time the Gospels talked about Peter being near a coal fire is when he was in the courtyard of the high priest's house during Jesus' trial. Around that coal fire, Peter distinctly and adamantly denied being Jesus' disciple three times (John 18:18). Maybe Peter thought of that shameful moment as he ate with Jesus around the coal fire.

During the Last Supper, Peter had promised to follow Jesus under any circumstances, even if that meant laying down his life for Jesus (John 13:37). Later that same night, however, Peter denied even knowing him (John 18:15–18, 25–27). The realization of the contradiction between professing loyalty and then denying Jesus drove Peter to weep bitterly (Matt. 26:25). God's kingdom, however, is all about restoration. On this day, after the disciples consumed the fish and bread, Jesus asked Peter three different times if Peter truly loved him. When Jesus asked a third time, Peter was grieved. Potentially, his grief stemmed from the memory of denying Jesus three times. On the beach in Galilee, Jesus restored his disciple by having him verbally affirm three times his love for Jesus. Jesus then commissioned that lifelong fisherman to become a shepherd of God's flock. Jesus asked Peter to follow his example as the good shepherd (cf. John 10:11–16; Isa. 40:11) and to be a leader for those in his care. The responsibility came with the acknowledgement that, as Peter had promised Jesus at the Passover supper, following Jesus' example would mean laying down his life (John 21:18–19).

Post-Resurrection: Acts

Each Gospel, except Luke, ends its narrative with Jesus commissioning his followers to go and "make disciples of all nations, baptizing them in the name of the Father and of the Son and the of Holy Spirit, and teaching them to obey everything I have commanded you" (Matt. 28:19–20). Luke, however, wrote a second book to carry on the narrative. While you may think that the end of the Gospels seems like the proper place to end this book about Jesus, Luke makes an important connection in the first part of Acts that will help us understand the spread of the gospel story into the rest of the world.

The book of Acts opens in Jerusalem forty days after the resurrection. Jesus told the disciples to remain in the city until the Holy Spirit came upon them. At that time, they would become witnesses in Jerusalem, Judea, Samaria, and to the ends of the earth (Acts 1:8). Then Jesus ascended into heaven and was gone.

In this part of the narrative, the reader comes across an unspoken assumption and we need to do a little detective work to uncover it. Think about the timing of all these events. Jesus died during Passover, and Jesus spent forty days with his disciples. Do you know what time of year it was when Jesus ascended into heaven? If necessary, go back and read chapter 2 to remind yourself of the agricultural calendar and how it is paired with the religious holidays. Passover was celebrated in March/April. The people then counted seven weeks, or forty-nine days, until the next holiday, which came at the end of the wheat harvest. Since each holiday was filled with significant memories of what God did in the lives of Israelites, you should be asking yourself what this second holiday represented.

Forty-nine days after Passover, the Jews celebrated Shavuot, which was a time to remember the covenant that God made with his people at Mount Sinai. Part of the detective work is to ask yourself what images and sounds were used to describe the Israelite experience at Mount Sinai. The book of Exodus says that God showed up as a theophany: wind, fire, clouds, and trumpet blasts (Exod. 19:16–19). God gave Moses instructions for life so the Israelites could become a nation that honored God, but then the story of the golden calf punctures this Sinai story with a consequence of the death of three thousand Israelites (Exod. 32).

Notice that when Jesus ascended into heaven, he had been with his followers for forty days. That means they were nine days away from Shavuot. They returned to the city and waited for what would come next. Acts 2:1 says, "When the day of Pentecost came." The word *Pentecost* comes from the Greek word that means "fiftieth." The day of Pentecost was Shavuot! And suddenly those followers of Jesus who were gathered together in one place were filled with the Holy Spirit. But notice how the Holy Spirit appears. The place was engulfed by loud sounds, a cloud, and tongues of fire. The imagery helps the reader make a connection across time. Shavuot reminded the people of the grace of God when he gave the Torah to Israel at Mount Sinai. Now on Shavuot, using similar theophanic images, God gave the Holy Spirit to the church (2:1–4).

The book of Acts continues by saying, "Now there were staying in Jerusalem God-fearing Jews from every nation under heaven" (2:5). Why were so many different people in Jerusalem? For Shavuot! These were God-fearing Jews, who lived in different lands but who made the journey to Jerusalem to celebrate this significant holiday at God's temple. According to Acts 2:9–11, people in the crowd came from the far reaches of the Roman Empire, including Egypt and northern Africa. They were astonished to hear the "Galileans" speaking multiple languages (2:6–7).

Peter stood up and began to address the crowd: "Fellow Jews and all of you who live in Jerusalem . . . " (v. 14). He continued by interpreting that day's events with segments from the prophet Joel. You know from previous chapters that when New Testament writers quote from the Old Testament, the entire context of the quote matters for understanding the message in the New Testament.

Joel warned the Israelites about the ramifications of continuing to ignore their covenant with God. He used dramatic and visual language about an infestation of locusts and swarming armies that would annihilate the Israelites. Joel called the people to repent, and he promised that if they returned to God, then God would respond by restoring what the armies and the locusts had destroyed. Joel continued with a vision of what the restored kingdom would look like:

"And afterward,
　　I will pour out my Spirit on all people.
Your sons and daughters will prophesy,
　　your old men will dream dreams,
　　your young men will see visions.
Even on my servants, both men and women,
　　I will pour out my Spirit in those days." (Joel 2:28–29)

In response to questions from the Jerusalem crowd, Peter drew a connection between the writings of Joel and the events of that day. Restoration happened through Jesus, and now God had poured out his Spirit on all of his people. Peter continued with two psalms (Pss. 16 and 110), which are both attributed to David. In this skillfully crafted speech, Peter used insider language with those who recognized the portions of Scripture he quoted within their larger context. The primarily Jewish crowd was knowledgeable about Israelite/Jewish history, their Scriptures, and their hope for restoration. Peter took this insider knowledge and used it to demonstrate how Jesus—his death and resurrection—made sense of the larger idea of the kingdom of God. People were astonished by his words. Those who believed were baptized into the new covenant. Do you want to guess how many were baptized that day? Three thousand! The same number of Israelites who died at Sinai after the golden calf incident. The process of restoration was still under way.

The early Jewish-Christian movement was a kingdom of God movement. People continued to go to the temple, but they also met in each other's homes, and the movement spread quickly (3:45–47).

Spreading the News[2]

Understanding Jesus' life and mission is intertwined with knowing Israelite Scriptures and the geographical places of historic events. Yet Jesus told the disciples to spread the news of God's kingdom from Jerusalem to Judea, Samaria, and the ends of the earth. These instructions are sometimes explained in churches and Bible studies as geographical references moving in concentric circles from the smallest location to the next larger location. That is only partially true. If the instructions were only geographical, you would expect Jesus to say, "Jerusalem, Judea, Samaria, and *Galilee*"—especially given how much time Jesus spent in Galilee. But Galilee is omitted and replaced with "the ends of the earth." This is a clue to the underlying cultural meaning of the instructions. Each listed name is more than a geographical marker. The name identifies a different way of seeing the world, and their nuanced meaning deserves careful attention.

Jerusalem

Jerusalem was the focal point of the Davidic kingdom. During the Babylonian exile, the Jewish people held onto the hope of Jerusalem being restored and lifted up high among the mountains to draw all nations to it. When the Jews were allowed to return to their ancestral land, Jerusalem was the first city they rebuilt. Most importantly, this city was where the one and only temple to the living God was built, which represented the garden-like place where humans could be in the sacred presence of God.

The combination of the historical and religious significance of Jerusalem and the temple creates the anchor point of the gospel message, as well as the key starting point for the spread of the good news. The Holy Spirit came upon those waiting in the upper room, and crowds of Jewish people gathered to investigate the unusual event. You many think that if they all took Peter's message home with them, then the message reached the "ends of the earth." However, all the people in the crowd were ideologically focused on the Jerusalem temple, so that spread would not represent a changed world. Additionally, the early chapters of Acts focus only on events in and around the temple. As long as the message stayed in Jerusalem, it inhabited a Jewish, temple-centric story.

Judea

The Gospels record Jesus' interactions with the people in Judea, but most of those activities were in or around Jerusalem.[3] In chapter 5, we talked about how Jesus received significant resistance from the Judeans, which may be due in part to the mountainous terrain. The geographical obstacles restricted interactions with outsiders and thus limited the challenges to conservative social views. This conservative worldview of the Judeans, along with the "ivory tower" reputation of the scholars at the Jerusalem temple, may have led to the resistance Jesus faced when in Judea.

News of the resurrection of Jesus and the completion of God's restoration spread. Acts 5 says the people from surrounding towns in Judea went to Jerusalem to see what was happening. The communities that had previously resisted Jesus were now seeking explanations for what they heard.

Samaria

Moving the good news out of Jerusalem to the surrounding country-side retains the implication of a primarily Jewish audience that shared a similar worldview and knowledge of Scriptures. Communicating the core Jewish ideas of restoration would be more difficult with the next move to Samaria.

Although the geographical regions of Judea and Samaria were considered one political unit by Rome, they were not considered unified by the people who lived there. These people groups, and the terrain in which they lived, held memories of the past that reinforced the separation between populations. There were memories of a divided Israelite kingdom and Assyrian and Babylonian exiles that influenced the Israelites in different ways (you can refresh your memory about these details in chapter 1). The Samaritans and the returning Jews from exile clashed over the building of the Jerusalem temple, and this animosity remained for centuries, growing deeper and deeper roots in their communities.

Despite the historic rivalry, the Gospel of Luke records how Jesus purposefully interacted with the Samaritans (Luke 9:52–54; 10:33–37; 17:11–19). Through his life and teachings, Jesus demonstrated to his disciples how the gospel message included the Samaritans along with the Jews. The book of Acts continues this message. A great persecution hit the young Christian community in Jerusalem and forced people to flee to the surrounding areas. Samaritan villages were impacted greatly (Acts 8:1, 4–25).

Ends of the Earth

The final geographical designation was the "ends of the earth." This last area dismantled any thought about restrictions on restored space. God's kingdom was not just for the people of Israel, even if Jerusalem was at the head.[4] To reach the "ends of the earth," the disciples needed to breach the ethnic divides that historically defined Israel's space.[5]

The difficult act of translation also began. The book of Acts records how the early church struggled with how to take a story grounded in the rocks, soil, and scenery of Judea and Galilee and translate it to a people in a place different from their own. Acts 15 records a pivotal argument at the council meeting in Jerusalem when Paul returned from a missionary trip to report what was happening abroad. Some Pharisees, who were believers, suggested that all believing Gentiles must be circumcised and required to follow the Torah (Acts 15:5). Only after much discussion did the leaders decide that since the Holy Spirit was being poured out on the Gentiles in the same way that the Holy Spirit was poured out on the Jews, then God must not require Gentiles to become Jewish, and so neither would they. With that decision, the focus of the book of Acts shifts from Peter to Paul. Paul traveled throughout the Roman Empire and took the story of Jesus to those who did not know the Israelite narrative, much less their sacred text. Through Paul, the message of God's kingdom spread beyond the Jews to the Gentiles.

Conclusion

While the book of Acts follows the expansion theme, there remains a consistent return to that which anchors the gospel message. Although the good news flowed out to other places, it also connected those audiences back to the core of Jerusalem and to the life, death, and resurrection of Jesus. Gentiles living throughout the Roman Empire did not have the same narrative, history, or memory preserved in their surrounding landscapes, but they were invited to acknowledge all that was preserved in the Jewish story. The Holy Spirit empowered the disciples to move outward and to ultimately include the Gentiles, because no boundary limited the restoration offered by God's kingdom. But the story of restoration would always be fully embedded in the events in Jerusalem.

I want to draw your attention again to Psalm 22. In the last chapter, we talked about the significance of this psalm as Jesus' final words on the cross (Mark 15:34; Matt. 27:46). The opening words he quoted identified the psalm to the listeners, who likely had the whole psalm memorized. Psalm 22 laments the isolation, pain, and injustice happening to the speaker, but it ends with a grand proclamation of faith in the ultimate victory of God. Read these words from verses 26–31 in light of the aftermath of Jesus' resurrection and the spread of the good news to the ends of the earth:

> The poor will eat and be satisfied;
>   those who seek the Lord will praise him—
>   may your hearts live forever!
> All the ends of the earth
>   will remember and turn to the Lord,
> and all the families of the nations
>   will bow down before him,

for dominion belongs to the Lord
>and he rules over the nations.
All the rich of the earth will feast and worship;
>all who go down to the dust will kneel before him—
>those who cannot keep themselves alive.
Posterity will serve him;
>future generations will be told about the Lord.
They will proclaim his righteousness,
>declaring to a people yet unborn:
>He has done it!

Although Jesus died with the first line of this psalm on his lips, it ends with a declaration that all nations will witness that God is on his throne:

Future generations will be told about the Lord.

You are those future generations! And the final declaration of this psalm is that every generation will continue to proclaim all that God set out to do through the life and resurrection of Jesus. It is now *your* turn to shift from learning about the life of Jesus to taking on the challenge to share the life of Jesus with the world!

Notes

Introduction

1. See E. Randolph Richards and Brandon J. O'Brien, *Misreading Scripture with Western Eyes: Removing Cultural Blinders to Better Understand the Bible* (Downers Grove, IL: InterVarsity Press, 2012); and Marvin R. Wilson, *Our Father Abraham: Jewish Roots of the Christian Faith* (Grand Rapids: Eerdmans, 1989), 23–29.

2. Wilson, *Our Father Abraham*, 139.

3. Wilson, *Our Father Abraham*, 138.

4. Wilson, *Our Father Abraham*, 185.

5. See Wilson's excellent discussion in *Our Father Abraham*, 39–103.

6. We will discuss this further in chapter 10.

7. See chapters 3 and 5 for the development of different expressions of Judaism.

8. For a discussion of the social and national process of separation between the Jews and Jewish Christians, see David Flusser, "The Jewish-Christian Schism (Part II)," *Immanuel* 17 (Winter, 1983/84): 30–39; and Wilson, *Our Father Abraham*, 64–73.

9. Wilson, *Our Father Abraham*, 78.

10. Flusser, "The Jewish-Christian Schism (Part II)," 35.

11. For an explanation of the long history of anti-Semitism in the church, see Wilson, *Our Father Abraham*, 87–103.

12. Richard B. Hays, *Echoes of Scripture in the Gospels* (Waco, TX: Baylor University Press, 2016), 5.

13. The Old Testament (Hebrew Bible) and the Greek translation of the Hebrew Bible are invaluable, but other Jewish writings were produced between 200 BCE and 100 CE that are not included in the Hebrew Bible. These are helpful for determining the primary issues that the Jewish community was debating at the time. The Dead Sea Scrolls are also important not only for the copies of the Hebrew Bible and the Septuagint, but for their inclusion of other Jewish writings that help us understand the Judaism(s) reflected in the Gospels. Also helpful are the Jewish historians like Philo of Alexandria (20 BCE–40 CE) and Josephus (37–100 CE). Finally, there is a wealth of rabbinic literature that was codified long after the life of Jesus but presents an insider's view on the best of Jewish scholarship and thought. See Wilson, *Our Father Abraham*, 30–31.

Chapter 1

1. Hays, *Echoes of Scripture in the Gospels*, 5.

2. Details regarding Jewish education are discussed in chapter 5.

3. Hays, *Echoes of Scripture in the Gospels*, 5.

4. Hays, *Echoes of Scripture in the Gospels*, 1–6.

5. All Bible citations are from the NIV unless otherwise noted.

6. See G. J. Wenham, "Sanctuary Symbolism in the Garden of Eden Story," *Proceedings of the World Congress of Jewish Studies* 9 (1986): 399–404; and G. K. Beale and Mitchell Kim, *God Dwells among Us: Expanding Eden to the Ends of the Earth* (Downers Grove, IL: InterVarsity Press, 2014), 17–28.

7. Pinchas Lapide and Peter Stuhlmacher, *Paul: Rabbi and Apostle*, trans. Lawrence W. Denef (Minneapolis: Augsburg, 1984), 37–39. Quoted from Wilson, *Our Father Abraham*, 21.

8. Wilson, *Our Father Abraham*, 33.

9. See Cyndi Parker, "A Geographical Analysis of the Steps Undertaken by David in the Consolidation of His Rule over All Israel," in *Lexham Geographic Commentary on the Historical Books*, vol. 2, ed. Barry J. Beitzel (Bellingham, WA: Lexham Press, 2020).

10. Wilson, *Our Father Abraham*, 119.

11. Christopher Wright, *Knowing Jesus through the Old Testament*, 2nd ed. (Downers Grove, IL: InterVarsity Press, 2014), 115.

Chapter 2

1. For a more detailed description of the geographical context of this event, see Cyndi Parker, "The People's Thirst at the Feast of Tabernacles," in *Lexham Geographic Commentary on the Gospels,* ed. Barry J. Beitzel (Bellingham, WA: Lexham Press, 2017), 356–64.

Chapter 3

1. See Lee Martin McDonald, *Formation of the Bible: The Story of the Church's Canon* (Peabody, MA: Hendrickson, 2012).

2. See Irina Frasin, "Greeks, Barbarians and Alexander the Great: The Formula for an Empire," *Athens Journal of History.* 5, no. 3 (July 2019): 209–24.

3. Isocrates, *Panegyricus*, 50.

4. A detailed explanation of the influence of Hellenism as a cultural force is in Martin Hengel, *Judaism and Hellenism: Studies in their Encounter in Palestine during the Early Hellenistic Period*, trans. John Bowden (Eugene, OR: Wipf & Stock, 1974), 58–78.

5. For a detailed look at the political and military exploits of this war, see Robin Waterfield, *Dividing the Spoils: The War for Alexander the Great's Empire* (Oxford: Oxford University Press, 2011).

6. The Greek translation of the Hebrew Bible, the Septuagint, was commissioned in Egypt by Ptolemy II for the library in Alexandra. The Septuagint proved essential for the Jews living in Egypt who no longer spoke Hebrew. When the entirety of Scripture was translated, it was distributed to Jews throughout the diaspora. For an excellent introduction to the Septuagint, see Karen Jobes and Moisés Silva, *Invitation to the Septuagint* (Grand Rapids: Baker Academic, 2000).

7. See N. T. Wright, *The New Testament and the People of God* (Minneapolis: Fortress Press, 1992), 215–43.

8. Polybius, 26.10.

9. See deSilva's discussion on "The Saviors of Israel," in David A. deSilva, *An Introduction to the New Testament: Contexts, Methods & Ministry Formation* (Downers Grove, IL: InterVarsity Press, 2004), 46–50.

10. A chief aim of the Pharisees was to educate all the people in Torah. They believed that even if the high priest and political elite embraced Hellenism as a cultural movement, an educated population would be equipped to resist it. See Hengel, *Judaism and Hellenism*, 78–83.

11. She was admired so much that later Jewish writings claim that during her rule, rain fell only on the Sabbath so that the working class suffered no loss of pay from the rain falling during their worktime. The fertility of the soil was so great that the grains of wheat grew as large as kidney beans, barley as large as olives, and lentils as like gold denars. See Jacob Neusner, *The Rabbinic Traditions about the Pharisees Before 70, Part 1: The Masters* (Leiden: E. J. Brill, 1971), 106. See also Kenneth Atkinson, "The Salome No One Knows: Long-time Ruler of a Prosperous and Peaceful Judea Mentioned in Dead Sea Scrolls," *Biblical Archaeology Review* 34, no. 4 (July/August 2008): 60–65, 72–73.

12. The Idumeans were people with ancestral ties to the Edomites, a people with a long rivalry with the Israelites stretching all the way back to Jacob and Esau.

13. Josephus, *Antiquities of the Jews,* 14.69–73.

14. Josephus, *Antiquities,* 14.9.1

Chapter 4

1. N. T. Wright, *Jesus and the Victory of God* (Minneapolis: Fortress Press, 1996), 483.

2. Cyndi Parker, "Crossing to 'The Other Side' of the Sea of Galilee," in *Lexham Geographic Commentary on the Gospels* (Bellingham, WA: Lexham Press, 2017), 157–64.

Chapter 5

1. For pictures and explanations of the Jerusalem palaces, see Nahman Avigad, *Discovering Jerusalem* (Nashville: Thomas Nelson, 1983).

2. Jodi Magness, *Stone and Dung, Oil and Spit: Jewish Life in the Time of Jesus* (Grand Rapids: Eerdmans, 2011), 13–14.

3. Carol Meyers, *Rediscovering Eve: Ancient Israelite Women in Context* (Oxford: Oxford University Press, 2013); and Lynn H. Cohick, *Women in the World of the Earliest Christians: Illuminating Ancient Ways of Life* (Grand Rapids: Baker Academic, 2009).

4. Cohick, *Women in the World of the Earliest Christians*, 225–55.

5. Cohick, *Women in the World of the Earliest Christians*, 217–18; Bernadette J. Brooten, *Women Leaders in the Ancient Synagogue*, BJS 36 (Atlanta: Scholars Press, 1982).

6. Cohick, *Women in the World of the Earliest Christians*, 195–224.

7. Wilson, *Our Father Abraham*, 289–90.

8. Abraham J. Heschel, *Insecurity of Freedom: Essays on Human Existence* (New York: Schocken Books, 1972), 41. Cf. Wilson, *Our Father Abraham*, 291.

9. Josephus, *Against Apion*, 1.60.

10. William Barclay, *Educational Ideals in the Ancient World* (Grand Rapids: Baker Books, 1980), 12–13.

11. Shmuel Safrai and M. Stern, eds., *The Jewish People in the First Century: Historical Geography, Political History, Social, Cultural, and Religious Life*, vol. 2 (Philadelphia: Fortress Press, 1987), 964.

12. Jacob Neusner, *A Life of Yohanan ben Zakkai Ca. 1–80 C. E.*, 2nd ed. (Leiden: Brill, 1970), 97.

13. David Daube, *The New Testament and Rabbinic Judaism* (Peabody, MA: Hendrickson, 1998), 205–7.

14. Jim R. Sibley, "Jewish Groups in the First Century," in *A Handbook on the Jewish Roots of the Christian Faith,* ed. Craig A. Evans and David Mishkin (Peabody, MA: Hendrickson, 2019), 124–25.

15. Sibley, "Jewish Groups in the First Century," 124–25.

16. Sibley, "Jewish Groups in the First Century," 124–25.

17. N. T. Wright, *Jesus and the Victory of God*, 418.

18. Josephus, *Antiquities*, 18.9.

Chapter 6

1. For good comparisons between the Gospel birth narratives, see Kenneth E. Bailey, *Jesus through Middle Eastern Eyes* (Downers Grove, IL: IVP Academic, 2008); Barry J. Beitzel, ed., *Lexham Geographic Commentary on the Gospels* (Bellingham, WA: Lexham Press, 2017); and Jeannine K. Brown, *Matthew* (Grand Rapids: Baker Books, 2015).

2. Think of Boaz, who lived in Bethlehem and had fields of grain. His great grandson, David, was a shepherd. Additionally, the prophet Amos was a farmer and a shepherd from the neighboring evillage of Tekoa.

3. For an in-depth discussion of the significance of kinship and how that influences reading New Testament text, see David A. deSilva, *Honor, Patronage, Kinship and Purity: Unlocking New Testament Culture* (Downers Grove, IL: InterVarsity Press, 2000), esp. 157–240.

4. For more details, see Cyndi Parker, "The Geography of the David and Bathsheba Incident," in *Lexham Geographic Commentary on the Historical Books,* ed. Barry J. Beitzel (Bellingham, WA: Lexham Press, 2016).

5. See Raymond E. Brown, *The Birth of the Messiah: A Commentary on the Infancy Narratives in Matthew and Luke,* new updated ed. (New York: Doubleday, 1993), 71–74.

6. In fact, the two genealogies include similar facts only about one-third of the time, which simply emphasizes the Gospel writer's way of painting a portrait of Jesus.

7. C. Wright, *Knowing Jesus through the Old Testament,* 63–108.

8. Herodotus, *Histories* 1.101, 107, 120; 3.65, 73, 79; 7.19, 37, 113.

9. For a detailed explanation of the historical placement of the census mentioned by Luke, see Brown, *The Birth of the Messiah,* 547–56.

10. We cannot assume they went the shortest way, because the road passed through Samaritan territory, and often the Jews tried to avoid Samaritan regions.

11. John J. Rousseau and Rami Arav, *Jesus and His World: An Archaeological and Cultural Dictionary* (Minneapolis: Fortress Press, 1995), 128–31; Yizhar Hirschfeld, *The Palestinian Dwelling in the Roman-Byzantine Period* (Jerusalem: Franciscan Press, 1995), 21–107.

12. See the extended conversation in Cohick, *Women in the World of the Earliest Christians,* 152–56.

13. Rabbinic sources state there were fields to the southeast of Bethlehem dedicated to raising animals offered as sacrifices at the temple. It is supposed that these shepherds were more ritually pure than normal shepherds and therefore may have been the ones the angels address. This is a tempting interpretation, especially since John calls Jesus "the Lamb of God" (John 1:29), but it cannot be adequately proven.

14. One inscription about Caesar Augustus describes him as "son of a god, imperator of land and sea, the benefactor and savior of the whole world."

Chapter 7

1. Cf. C. Wright, *Knowing Jesus through the Old Testament,* esp. 109–41.

2. Josephus describes John's attitude toward baptism in *Antiquity* 18:117.

3. C. Wright, *Knowing Jesus through the Old Testament,* 147.

4. Traditionally translated as "Red Sea," but the text is referring to a smaller body of water more accurately named the Reed Sea.

5. For a great discussion about how the Old Testament formed Jesus' understanding of his mission, see C. Wright, *Knowing Jesus through the Old Testament,* 109–83.

6. C. Wright, *Knowing Jesus through the Old Testament,* 184–93.

7. The Gospels list the final two temptations in different orders, but Jesus' responses remain the same. The order I use here comes from the Gospel of Matthew.

8. The geographical significance of this move was discussed in chapter 2.

9. C. Wright, *Knowing Jesus through the Old Testament,* 151.

Chapter 8

1. For a longer discussion of Jesus' use of nature images, see Vernon Alexander, "The Words and Teachings of Jesus in the Context of Galilee," in *Lexham Geographic Commentary on the Gospels,* ed. Barry J. Beitzel (Bellingham, WA: Lexham Press, 2017), 134–48.

2. See Elaine A. Phillips, "Jesus' Interpretation of Weather Patterns," in *Lexham Geographic Commentary on the Gospels,* ed. Barry J. Beitzel (Bellingham, WA: Lexham Press, 2017), 278–85.

3. Richard A. Horsley, "Jesus and Galilee: The Contingencies of a Renewal Movement," in *Galilee through the Centuries: Confluence of Cultures*, ed. Eric M. Meyers (Winona Lake, IN: Eisenbrauns, 1999), 63.

4. A wonderful example of this is in Henri Nouwen, *The Return of the Prodigal Son: A Story of Homecoming* (New York: Doubleday, 1992).

5. See Danielle Parish, "Jesus' Reference to Folklore and Historical Events," *Jerusalem Perspective* (June 2006), https://www.jerusalemperspective.com/4446.

6. Brad Young, *The Parables: Jewish Tradition and Christian Interpretation* (Peabody, MA: Hendrickson Publishers, 1998), 16.

7. Wilson, *Our Father Abraham*, 181.

8. Wilson, *Our Father Abraham*, 174.

9. Wilson, *Our Father Abraham*, 175.

Chapter 9

1. See chapter 4 for the discussion of previous messiahs who appeared after Herod the Great's death, along with the Roman massacre of Jews during a previous Passover celebration.

2. For an in-depth discussion of this event, see Nicholas Perrin, *Jesus the Temple* (London: SPCK; Grand Rapids: Baker Academic, 2010), 92–113.

3. "Blood of the covenant" refers to the Sinai covenant in Exodus 24:8. Jesus' use of the phrase in the Gospels means that Jesus' blood seals the new covenant between God and the people. The phrase may also be an allusion to Zechariah 9:11, an interesting connection especially in the Gospel of Matthew, who makes an earlier reference to Zechariah 9:9. Zechariah offers messianic hope for the king who will reign and set God's people free and rule peacefully. "Matthew's last supper scene creates a complex overlay of intertextual echoes, recalling both the blood-spattered covenantal banquet of Exodus 24 and the blood-secured messianic promise of deliverance found in Zechariah 9." Hays, *Echoes of Scripture in the Gospels,* 135.

4. For details see Avigad, *Discovering Jerusalem.*

5. During the Hasmonean dynasty the Sanhedrin had extensive authority and was a partner in government, but Herod limited its activity and role in government. The Sanhedrin was permitted to function as Jewish court, but the Roman governor of Jerusalem had the final say. See N. T. Wright, *Jesus,* 519–28.

6. N. T. Wright, *Jesus and the Victory of God,* 483.

7. Hays, *Echoes of Scripture in the Gospels*, 151.

8. For a detailed description of Pilate, see Helen K. Bond, *Pontius Pilate in History and Interpretation*, SNTSMS 100 (Cambridge: Cambridge University Press, 1998).

9. N. T. Wright, *Jesus and the Victory of God*, 543–47.

Chapter 10

1. Geographically identifying Emmaus is challenging for modern scholars, and four sites are suggested as possible locations of the ancient city. No matter which site is correct, however, the disciples would still have to walk down the steep western slope of the Judean hills. Details of the speculations behind the location of Emmaus are available in Anson Rainey and R. Steven Notley, *The Sacred Bridge* (Jerusalem: Carta, 2006), 367–68.

2. For more detail than what I explain here, please see Cyndi Parker, "The Threefold Expansion of the Early Church: Jerusalem, Judea, and Samaria," in *Lexham Geographic Commentary on Acts through Revelation*, ed. Barry J. Beitzel (Bellingham, WA: Lexham Press, 2019), 42–50.

3. For a detailed discussion of Jesus' interactions in Judea, see Chris McKinny, "The Words and Teachings of Jesus in the Context of Judea," in *Lexham Geographic Commentary on the Gospels*, ed. by Barry J. Beitzel (Bellingham, WA: Lexham Press, 2017), 338–55.

4. Matthew Sleeman, *Geography and the Ascension Narrative in Acts* (Cambridge: Cambridge University Press, 2009), 70.

5. Sleeman, *Geography and the Ascension Narrative in Acts*, 71.

RECOMMENDED READING

Bailey, Kenneth E. *Jesus through Middle Eastern Eyes: Cultural Studies in the Gospels.* Downers Grove, IL: IVP Academic, 2008.

Beitzel, Barry J., ed. *Lexham Geographic Commentary on the Gospels.* Bellingham, WA: Lexham Press, 2016.

deSilva, David A. *Introducing the Apocrypha: Message, Content and Significance.* Grand Rapids, MI: Baker Academic, 2002.

Green, Joel B., and Lee Martin McDonald, eds. *The World of the New Testament: Cultural, Social, and Historical Contexts.* Grand Rapids: Baker Academic, 2013.

Hayes, Richard B. *Echoes of Scripture in the Gospels.* Waco, TX: Baylor University Press, 2016.

Imes, Carmen Joy. *Bearing God's Name: Why Sinai Still Matters.* Downers Grove, IL: InterVarsity Press, 2019.

Levine, Amy-Jill Levine. *Short Stories by Jesus: The Enigmatic Parables of a Controversial* Rabbi. New York: HarperOne, 2014.

Magness, Jodi. *Stone and Dung, Oil and Spit: Jewish Daily Life in the Time of Jesus.* Grand Rapids: Eerdmans, 2011.

Richards, E. Randolph, and Brandon J. O'Brien. *Misreading Scripture with Western Eyes: Removing Cultural Blinders to Better Understand the Bible.* Downers Grove, IL: InterVarsity Press, 2012.

Richter, Sandra L. *The Epic of Eden: A Christian Entry into the Old Testament.* Downers Grove, IL: InterVarsity Press, 2008.

Snodgrass, Klyne R. *Stories with Intent: A Comprehensive Guide to the Parables of Jesus.* Grand Rapids: Eerdmans, 2008.

Wright, Christopher. *Knowing Jesus through the Old Testament.* 2nd ed. Downers Grove, IL: InterVarsity Press, 2014.

Young, Brad H. *Jesus the Jewish Theologian.* Peabody, MA: Hendrickson, 1995.

———. *Meet the Rabbis: Rabbinic Thought and the Teachings of* Jesus. Peabody, MA: Hendrickson, 2007.

Zuck, Roy B. *Teaching as Jesus Taught.* Grand Rapids: Baker Books, 1995.

Bibliography

Alexander, Vernon. "The Words and Teachings of Jesus in the Context of Galilee." In *Lexham Geographic Commentary on the Gospels*, edited by Barry J. Beitzel, 134–48. Bellingham, WA: Lexham Press, 2017.

Atkinson, Kenneth. "The Salome No One Knows: Long-time Ruler of a Prosperous and Peaceful Judea Mentioned in Dead Sea Scrolls." *Biblical Archaeology Review* 34, no. 4 (July/August 2008): 60–65, 72–73.

Avigad, Nahman. *Discovering Jerusalem*. Nashville: Thomas Nelson, 1983.

Bailey, Kenneth E. *Jesus through Middle Eastern Eyes: Cultural Studies in the Gospels*. Downers Grove, IL: IVP Academic, 2008.

Barclay, William. *Educational Ideals in the Ancient World*. Grand Rapids: Baker Books, 1980.

Beale, G. K. and Mitchell Kim. *God Dwells among Us: Expanding Eden to the Ends of the Earth*. Downers Grove, IL: InterVarsity Press, 2014.

Beitzel, Barry J., ed. *Lexham Geographic Commentary on the Gospels*. Bellingham, WA: Lexham Press, 2017.

Bond, Helen K. *Pontius Pilate in History and Interpretation*, SNTSMS 100. Cambridge: Cambridge University Press, 1998.

Brooten, Bernadette J. *Women Leaders in the Ancient Synagogue*, BJS 36. Atlanta: Scholars Press, 1982.

Brown, Jeannine K. *Matthew*. Teach the Text Commentary Series. Grand Rapids: Baker Books, 2015.

Brown, Raymond Edward. *The Birth of the Messiah: A Commentary on the Infancy Narratives in Matthew and Luke*, new updated ed. New York: Doubleday, 1993.

Cohick, Lynn H. *Women in the World of the Earliest Christians: Illuminating Ancient Ways of Life*. Grand Rapids: Baker Academic, 2009.

Daube, David. *The New Testament and Rabbinic Judaism*. Peabody, MA: Hendrickson, 1998.

deSilva, David A. *Introducing the Apocrypha: Message, Content and Significance*. Grand Rapids: Baker Academic, 2002.

———. *An Introduction to the New Testament: Contexts, Methods & Ministry Formation*. Downers Grove, IL: InterVarsity Press, 2004.

Flusser, David. "The Jewish-Christian Schism (Part II)." *Immanuel* 17 (Winter 1983/84): 30–39.

Frasin, Irina. "Greeks, Barbarians and Alexander the Great: The Formula for an Empire." *Athens Journal of History* 5, no. 3 (July 2019): 209–24.

Hays, Richard B. *Echoes of Scripture in the Gospels*. Waco, TX: Baylor University Press, 2016.

Hengel, Martin. *Judaism and Hellenism: Studies in their Encounter in Palestine during the Early Hellenistic Period*. Translated by John Bowden. Eugene, OR: Wipf & Stock, 1974.

Heschel, Abraham J. *Insecurity of Freedom: Essays on Human Existence*. New York: Schocken Books, 1972.

Hirschfeld, Yizhar. *The Palestinian Dwelling in the Roman-Byzantine Period*. Jerusalem: Franciscan Press, 1995.

Horsley, Richard A. "Jesus and Galilee: The Contingencies of a Renewal Movement." In *Galilee through the Centuries: Confluence of Cultures*, edited by Eric M. Meyers, 57–74. Winona Lake, IN: Eisenbrauns, 1999.

Imes, Carmen Joy. *Bearing God's Name: Why Sinai Still Matters*. Downers Grove, IL: InterVarsity Press, 2019.

Jobes, Karen, and Moisés Silva. *Invitation to the Septuagint*. Grand Rapids: Baker Academic, 2000.

Lapide, Pinchas, and Peter Stuhlmacher. *Paul: Rabbi and Apostle*. Translated by Lawrence W. Denef. Minneapolis: Augsburg, 1984.

Levine, Amy-Jill. *Short Stories by Jesus: The Enigmatic Parables of a Controversial Rabbi*. New York: HarperOne, 2014.

Magness, Jodi. *Stone and Dung, Oil and Spit: Jewish Life in the Time of Jesus*. Grand Rapids: Eerdmans, 2011.

McKinny, Chris. "The Words and Teachings of Jesus in the Context of Judea." In *Lexham Geographic Commentary on the Gospels*, edited by Barry J. Beitzel, 338–55. Bellingham, WA: Lexham Press, 2017.

Meyers, Carol. *Rediscovering Eve: Ancient Israelite Women in Context*. Oxford: Oxford University Press, 2013.

Neusner, Jacob. *A Life of Yohanan ben Zakkai Ca. 1–80 C. E.*, 2nd ed. Leiden: Brill, 1970.

———. *The Rabbinic Traditions about the Pharisees Before 70, Part 1: The Masters*. Leiden: E. J. Brill, 1971.

Parish, Danielle. "Jesus' Reference to Folklore and Historical Events," *Jerusalem Perspective* (June 2006). https://www.jerusalemperspective.com/4446.

Parker, Cyndi. "A Geographical Analysis of the Steps Undertaken by David in the Consolidation of His Rule Over All Israel." In *Lexham Geographic Commentary on the Historical Books*, edited by Barry J. Beitzel. Bellingham, WA: Lexham Press, 2020.

———. "The Geography of the David and Bathsheba Incident." In *Lexham Geographic Commentary on the Historical Books*, edited by Barry J. Beitzel. Bellingham, WA: Lexham Press, 2020.

———. "The People's Thirst at the Feast of Tabernacles." In *Lexham Geographic Commentary on the Gospels*, edited by Barry J. Beitzel, 356–64. Bellingham, WA: Lexham Press, 2017.

———. "The Threefold Expansion of the Early Church: Jerusalem, Judea, and Samaria." In *Lexham Geographic Commentary on Acts through Revelation*, edited by Barry J. Beitzel, 42–50. Bellingham, WA: Lexham Press, 2019.

Perrin, Nicholas. *Jesus the Temple*. London: SPCK; Grand Rapids: Baker Academic, 2010.

Phillips, Elaine A. "Jesus' Interpretation of Weather Patterns." In *Lexham Geographic Commentary on the Gospels*, edited by Barry J. Beitzel, 278–85. Bellingham, WA: Lexham Press, 2017.

Rainey, Anson, and R. Steven Notley, *The Sacred Bridge*. Jerusalem: Carta, 2006.

Richards, E. Randolph, and Brandon J. O'Brien. *Misreading Scripture with Western Eyes: Removing Cultural Blinders to Better Understand the Bible*. Downers Grove, IL: InterVarsity Press, 2012.

Richter, Sandra L. *The Epic of Eden: A Christian Entry into the Old Testament*. Downers Grove, IL: InterVarsity Press, 2008.

Rousseau, John J., and Rami Arav. *Jesus and His World: An Archaeological and Cultural Dictionary.* Minneapolis: Fortress Press, 1995.

Sleeman, Matthew. *Geography and the Ascension Narrative in Acts.* Cambridge: Cambridge University Press, 2009.

Sibley, Jim R. "Jewish Groups in the First Century." In *A Handbook on the Jewish Roots of the Christian Faith,* edited by Craig A. Evans and David Mishkin, 123–30. Peabody, MA: Hendrickson, 2019.

Snodgrass, Klyne R. *Stories with Intent: A Comprehensive Guide to the Parables of Jesus.* Grand Rapids: Eerdmans, 2008.

Waterfield, Robin. *Dividing the Spoils: The War for Alexander the Great's Empire.* Oxford: Oxford University Press, 2011.

Wenham, G. J. "Sanctuary Symbolism in the Garden of Eden Story." *Proceedings of the World Congress of Jewish Studies* 9 (1986): 399–404.

Wilson, Marvin R. *Our Father Abraham: Jewish Roots of the Christian Faith.* Grand Rapids: Eerdmans, 1989.

Wright, Christopher. *Knowing Jesus through the Old Testament,* 2nd ed. Downers Grove, IL: InterVarsity Press, 2014.

Wright, N. T. *Jesus and the Victory of God.* Minneapolis: Fortress Press, 1996.

———. *The New Testament and the People of God.* Minneapolis: Fortress Press, 1992.

Young, Brad H. *Jesus the Jewish Theologian.* Peabody, MA: Hendrickson, 1995.

Zuck, Roy B. *Teaching as Jesus Taught.* Grand Rapids: Baker Books, 1995.